Robert Fitterman
Creve Coeur

WITH AN AFTERWORD BY JOE MILUTIS

Winter Editions, 2024

CREVE COEUR

BOOK ONE

(2019)

Creve Coeur: Book 1

PREFACE

Rigor of beauty is what sort of quest and what for and for whom?
Why even speak of I, *he dreams, which interests me almost not at all?*

> To make a start: I come from a place
> called Creve Coeur, Missouri.
> *Creve Coeur*, loosely translated from the French
> as *broken heart*, a sleepy suburb of St. Louis.
> The name is derived from a dubious myth—
> a tortured love between an Osage woman
> and a French fur trapper, presumably
> ending with the woman's suicide. This same story
> is retold about a lot of midwestern lakes
> and it lands not too far from Disney's *Pocahontas*—
> number seven in the Disney princess line-up.
> Legend has it that when the lovers were torn apart,
> the woman leapt to her death from the waterfall
> into the bottom of Creve Coeur Lake.

The body of water, then, formed the shape
of a broken heart. *Hmm*, the face of the Falls cringes,
it's a story I've grown to live with.
A thin stream trickles

                    down the face
of the Falls, a far cry from the steps of the Uthina
amphitheater, slick with some vague
Missouri silt, moss, layers of green scum.
The Creve Coeur Falls has many names:
Dripping Springs, The Bluffs . . .
but it's more like a ledge than a waterfall—
it's neither very high nor impressive.
It never seemed ideal to me,
nor even possible, for a suicide—
lovesick or otherwise.

                    The Falls has its own
stories to tell: a corrupt
citizen's advisory committee on parks,
the 1917 race riots and massacre,
the infamous Pruitt-Igoe disaster,

the atrocities hatched at the Monsanto
Creve Coeur World Headquarters.

                    Power walking changes lives.
The best way to describe power walking
is to think of it as a low-impact alternative to jogging.
Basically, it takes regular walking and ups the intensity.
If you put two walkers next to each other,
and told one to move at a moderate pace
with their arms at their sides,
and told the other to increase their speed while
simultaneously pumping their arms—

    that's the technique!
Known in these parts, the Creve Coeur walker
powers up the sidewalks, at dusk, in the softest

of soft shoes, speeding past sleepy residents
who are still nestled in their soft bedrooms
                              in the softest homes
on earth. God willing.

                           Winding through the private
Monsanto service roads, he adjusts the volume
on his Walkman and looks out over the laboratories:
engineers, lawyers, chemists start to roll into the vast parking lot.
Swoosh! is the sound of the walker's poly-cotton track suit,

                           also called tipped fleece,
a deep burgundy offset nicely by his stark white
just-out-of-the-box New Balance.
He picks up his pace,

                           powering onto the sidewalk at Schnucks,
onward past McDonald's and into a future

                         Creve Coeur.

Schnucks: A Giant Among Supermarkets

I.

This is why I don't do self-checkout. I was at Schnucks with my dad and he was overcharged for two out of ten things. This happens almost every time we do self-checkout. My dad is somewhat hard of hearing, occasionally stubborn, so I get it when he insists on using self-checkout, but then I'm the one who has to stand in line at customer service and unload everything onto the counter. Ragu Pasta Sauce was three for $5. He got three but was charged $8. Chicken sausages were buy one, get one free. He got four and was charged for four. It's embarrassing
        and to top everything else off,
my dad was trying to return a bad batch of flowers, and since it wasn't
        on his Schnucks
Rewards Card they made him jump through hoops to exchange it.
My dad's a sweetheart but highly principled, and if crossed
he's been known to slam a bouquet of roses onto the service counter and
        everyone stands
around unaroused, like there's been *some misunderstanding.*

    —*Say it* . . . no ideas but
    the friendly faces of employees.
    Once upon a time, I worked at this Creve Coeur store
    and once when I was out back for a cigarette break,

    I set free a gold helium balloon trapped behind a dumpster.
    In bubbly cursive it read: *Best Day Ever*.

From above, higher than the Schnucks dumpsters
and the crumbling asphalt, higher than their rooftop,
high enough to make out the crack in the heart-shaped lake,
the shiny gold balloon, long hair flowing, an unrequited
love suicide, mangled in the dead leaves, plastic bags,
and dried weeds, a tiny man, ancient, shouting—
twisting in the wind, the other side of the balloon reads:
Grand Opening! Every new mall like a fresh start.

    Back then, there was a manager, Zach,
    who'd intentionally hide trash in corners
    to see if I was sweeping properly.
    Um . . . I think you missed this area.

A man like that, whose hair is very much in place,
like a tulip, knows how to bring an MBA degree
to grocery store management.

                             But Zach
was not a zip code unto himself.

  Zach used to boast that he's worked in nearly every Schnucks location, either helping out or training new hires. He's seen good store management and bad store management—it usually depended on the area.
  Zach claimed he wasn't prejudiced, but that the stores in North County, like in Ferguson or Spanish Lake, just weren't as up-to-speed as the ones in West County. He said that nearly every store had horrible deli department managers, except stores that had training locations—they always had top-notch deli managers, especially in Kirkwood and O'Fallon.
  Zach would tell horror stories about the deli departments, like when deli meats were dropped on the floor and then wiped off because the butchers felt that it was too much hassle to cut more. *Everything depended*, Zach said, *on the neighborhood*. Zach complained that the Union was taking too much money, but "Right To Work" failed horribly, so it wasn't his fault for voting it down.

Hands spinning like sparrows
at a small churchyard—
the buzz of the registers, the dance of the products,
the morning greetings, the coupons
held high in the air like auction bids—
all this will be replaced, Zach predicted.
He was torn, heartbroken really, by what
someone else might call progress.

Pretty soon, he'd lament, *there'll be no
such thing as a cashier or a bagger,
no small talk about the weather,
the Schnucks' flyer, new products, baseball—
like why the Cardinals need a real closer.*
Maybe Zach would miss all that, but not me:
I'm the suspicious, no-cart outsider.
The cashier figures that I'm stoned
on the catastrophe of descent, broken
wings, trampled, buying my single item,
arugula, held out like a prayer book—
the piercing light of a Presbyterian
chapel glowing from the eyes of the bagger.

What there is to learn (about how you got
what you got) is placed in the dark
pocket of a winter coat. That side-glance that
says you should be at the Whole Foods
in the other mall by Ballas Rd. I think of my dad
in these service industry situations,
a real pro, always a smile and a kind word
and yet this insistence on self-checkout—
the world is a strange

and unpredictable place. *What? I didn't steal anything!*
Once inside the car, the land dissolves into a slow-motion carousel

of the fine lawns juiced with Monsanto's best weed killer.
What's not to love? A tear rolls down the face of the Falls.
What is the best word to go with the sadness? Suffering,
we learn from love songs, is not the same as sorrow.

> The Falls will tell anyone who will listen what's hidden
> in the cracks of the limestone: promissory notes,
> eminent domain proposals, sleazy
> sub-prime mortgages.

   Manuel Lisa, or Manuel De Lisa, was both a Spanish and an American citizen. Around 1800, newly wed, he moved to St. Louis with his wife Polly after he obtained a land grant in the Missouri area. St. Louis, at this time, had a thriving fur trade established primarily by French colonists. Polly lived in the city with their three children while her husband Manuel made his long expeditions to various Indian territories on the Upper Missouri River. Soon after these successful expeditions, Manuel De Lisa established the Missouri Fur Company, together with prominent businessman and fur merchant Pierre Chouteau and William Clark, of Lewis & Clark notoriety. Mr. Lisa was soon appointed an Indian *subagent*, meaning he was authorized to trade with local Native American groups. During an expedition up the Missouri River into the Great Plains, working among the Omaha, Manual Lisa married Mitain—the daughter of Big Elk, their principal Chief and a renowned orator—even though he was still married to his first wife, Polly. It was not uncommon for men in the fur trade to marry Native American women because it helped solidify trade agreements between traders and local tribes.

> Once or twice a year I go back
> to Creve Coeur to visit my parents, and a few years ago
>   I helped move them
> out of their small suburban home with a yard
> and into an independent-living apartment building.
> The concept of the doggie-poop bag for their Cairn Terrier
> had to be introduced. I offered to go Schnucks.
> It was at least 100 degrees with no breeze.

In the bright breakfast cereal aisle
my shtetl relatives float, ghostly,
like cigar smoke, above the boxes: one proudly showing

his labor party card, another in a freshly ironed shirt
with his tie on, pushing a lawn mower across

a Honeycomb box, the rest of them huddled together
as in a home movie in their one-bedroom North St. Louis flat,
blinds closed, complaining about too much light—
I grew up thinking brightly lit homes equaled wealth.

I find a worker pricing soup cans
and ask where the doggy bags might be.
He looks at me bewildered: *take-out bags?*
No! Poop bags! I say, too loudly.
Oh, yeah, pretty sure we don't carry those.

      I wobble back to the Camry—
ARRGGHH! tiny gnats all over my face!

What does the miraculous look like?

Howard Phillip Venable was a renowned ophthalmologist from Detroit. He graduated from medical school with honors in 1940 and became the first African American to earn an ophthalmology degree from New York University. In 1943, Venable moved to St. Louis and practiced as an eye doctor at the all-Black Homer G. Phillips Hospital, which had a reputation for training some of the best nurses and doctors in the country. Glaucoma and cataracts were a big problem in Black communities, and Venable wanted to prepare his residents to work with Black patients specifically.

One day in March of 1956, Dr. Venable saw a small ad in a local newspaper, advertising 22 vacant lots in Creve Coeur, an all-white community, sparsely populated, with plenty of open space. Venable purchased two of the lots. He paid up-front, in cash, and set about building his ranch-style dream home. Then some of Venable's colleagues at the hospital got interested in the area too. Soon, several more Black families started making plans to buy lots in Creve Coeur. But achieving the suburban dream was never going to come easy. Right away, some of the white residents in Creve Coeur started organizing against Venable and the other Black families. They devised a wholesome looking plan with a sinister twist to keep their new neighbors out. They would build a park on the lots. And they quickly raised $25,000 amongst themselves to make it happen. This newly devised organization called itself the "Citizens Advisory Committee on Parks."

A wonder! A wonder!

    The committee's first proposal stated that the city should use its police power to take any property in cases where a group of citizens was willing to donate half the cost to turn property into a public park. In short, the committee had turned to eminent domain—which is supposed to be how the US government takes private property for public use, but in reality was a tool used to maintain segregation. Within weeks, this committee sued Dr. Venable and made several attempts to force him to surrender his property. Finally, he sold his new house to the county of Creve Coeur and started over.

> His ranch house (the Furies hurl!)
> reconfigured into a park
> clubhouse

    In 1961, Creve Coeur named the park Beirne Park, after the new mayor who was one of the original members of the Citizen Advisory Committee on Parks. Many years later, the Veneable family got a call from a labor lawyer in St. Louis who was writing an article about the history of the park for the Missouri Historical Society. In 2019, several activists and neighborhood organizers started working on a movement to rename the park after Dr. Venable. Court records showed that the residents leading to obtaining Dr. Venable's land were motivated by bigotry. After a town hall meeting with the mayor to discuss this history, the Creve Coeur city council voted unanimously to change the park's name: Beirne Park became Dr. H. Phillip Venable Memorial Park. Several members of the Venable family attended the event in person or by phone. Venable's niece, Rossalind Yvonne Venable Woodhouse, said: "so many people here are surprised. And I am among that group."

> Begin again! Next
> stop Krummenacher's Pharmacy—
> not because I have a good feeling
>   that they carry poop bags,
> but because there is a presence
>   that may or may not be greater . . .
> *Poop bags*? I'm directed

                to a shelf-stocking employee,
and I ask her if they carry doggie poop bags.
Wait what? she says, super friendly.
                Doggie poop bags, I repeat sheepishly.
Oh, follow me . . .
She leads me to the pet section . . .

        it's like we're wading
along the ocean floor.
        I lift my legs through
the underwater carpet—
finally we arrive at the impoverished
        pet supplies section.
        She scans the bar code under

the near empty shelf—*Oh no, sorry.*
        We're out.
At this point I need to rethink everything.
        PetCo! on the other side of I-270!
I head west on Ladue Rd. past the haves,
        whose futures look bright,
whose families have thrived
in the Ladue school district, then past
some forgotten '70s condo units, where two
        grown-ass men are
enjoying a front patio lounge

with Bud Light koozies: *Life is Sweet*
reads one T-shirt, *I Hate Everything*
        reads the other,
from the George Strait song?
        A kind of consolation prize,
or as my dad used to say,
a *constellation* prize!

If there was not beauty, there was a strangeness... these might have been the words of William Bartram, circa 1770, the botanist and travel writer who described the Native American territories and detailed the mounds in Cahokia, Illinois.

Around the twelfth century the largest city north of Mexico was Cahokia, sitting in what is now southern Illinois, across the Mississippi River from St. Louis. Built around 1050 and occupied through 1400, Cahokia had a population of between 25,000 and 50,000 people—similar to the population of London around this same era. The city of Cahokia is one of many large earthen mound complexes that dot the landscapes of the Ohio and Mississippi River Valleys and across the Southeast. Despite the preponderance of archaeological evidence that these mound complexes were the work of sophisticated Native American civilizations, this rich history has been obscured—or even buried—by the *Myth of the Mound Builders*: a narrative that arose ostensibly to explain the existence of the mounds.

Early white settlers and archaeologists were in such disbelief that these complex civilizations could have been constructed by Native Americans that they invented fantastical myths about their origins—ancient Norsemen, Toltecs, Vikings, Welshmen, Hindus, and even aliens were often cited as the builders of these mounds. It seemed that any group—other than the Native Americans—could serve as the likely architects of the great earthworks. These myths led to diminishing the achievements of pre-Columbian civilizations on the North American continent, just as the US government was expanding westward by taking control of Native American lands.

When William Bartram recorded these narratives of the mounds, he seemingly corroborated these mythical origin stories. Without any evidence, Bartram's early journals (*Travels*, 1791) suggest that the Creek and the Cherokee who lived around the mounds attributed their construction to "the ancients, many ages prior to their arrival and possessing of this country." Bartram's account of Creek and Cherokee histories leads to the view that these Native Americans were colonizers, just like the Euro-Americans. This served as one more way to justify the removal of Native Americans from their ancestral lands: if Native Americans were early colonizers, too, the logic went, then white Americans had just as much right to the land as indigenous peoples.

By 1400, the mounds were deserted. Theories regarding Cahokia's demise run the gamut from environmental disasters, to diseases, to political clashes with neighboring groups. Given the lack of concrete evidence, no one knows for sure. But one thing is certain: it was a gradual demise. There were over 25 mounds in downtown St. Louis. But by the late nineteenth century, all the mounds were dismantled to make room for some of the larger houses built around the era of the 1904 World's Fair. Even Big Mound, about the size of a football field and 34 feet high, was flattened.

On one especially sunny
morning at the kitchen table, my mom was pointing out
the *St. Louis Jewish Light* profile on Sophia M. Sachs

and the Butterfly House in Chesterfield—a township
just west of Creve Coeur, slightly newer,

                      more upscale, equally close to
Creve Coeur Park. Ms. Sachs, probably related
to the Sachs of Goldman-Sachs, sits on a log-bench
in front of her butterfly house. Proud, comfortable with her power,
hair frosted and coiffed tastefully, regal, smiling broadly.

Behind her, packed too tightly together,
is the staff of entomologists and administrators,
in a descending scale of freshness.

                      The Sophia M. Sachs Butterfly
House was named in honor of Sophia M. Sachs,
wife of the late Sam Sachs, who founded
Sachs Electric Company
and played a key role in the early real-estate
development of the suburbs west of St. Louis.

On the day we visited, we were surrounded
by an elementary school field trip—
most of the students had on high-end rain boots.
It was my mom's birthday, but because of the rain
she didn't get to experience the outdoor botanicals.

                      Our admission was free
thanks to our Schnucks coupon, so that the general
idea of value, like the rain, followed us.
The kids went wild under the glass dome—
toppling exotic green plants,

            grabbing at the tropical butterflies,
tossing aside their informational placards.
What separates them from us interests me a lot.

I found the reviews to be mixed. First of all, who is this Sachs? Is this family related to Goldman-Sachs? I wouldn't doubt it because the place isn't cheap, which is weird because you can see butterflies for free anywhere. And if you want to see exotic butterflies, they have them at the St Louis Zoo for free. At $8 a crack, it adds up—especially if you're, like, a family of five. My biggest complaint, though, was that the lady who sold me my ticket tried to keep my change (she was overly gushing about a cheap fake ring I had on), and then the lady in the gift shop kept trying to push me to buy more. I think I said, "no just the coloring book" about four times. She even walked away from the register to try and sell me other things.

The butterfly area was humid and enclosed, like a fancy bog greenhouse. Placards, with the butterfly types to locate, like a key, were a nice touch. The butterflies landed on the feeding stations. We walked along a path and the butterflies fluttered all around us! I don't know anything about butterflies, but my placard told me I should be surprised to see the orange and black spotted regal fritillary butterfly if I live on the East Coast, and since I do live on the East Coast, I suddenly felt surprised. Apparently, they are common in the Midwest but when spotted on the East Coast, it's a big deal. Like birders, butterfly enthusiasts bring their wide-angle lenses and make a trek to a butterfly sanctuary when the orange and black spotted regal fritillary are rumored to be migrating.

I'm reading these reviews about how great the butterfly house is for families and kids, but I think it's mixed. The kids looked horrified. The butterflies are all over them—in their hair, landing on their clothes. I'm not sure. Of course, some of the children are exuberant and delighted at having butterflies flutter around and land on their heads and on their arms. And a few children are studious and are completely oblivious to the butterflies because they're nose deep in pamphlets and books. And then, inevitably, there are a few anxious children hiding behind their parents. They flinch when the butterflies approach and shriek, *There are giant bugs FLYING AT MY FACE!* I feel for this last group of children, since I'm basically the taller, older version of them. Regardless of how beautiful these creatures are, it freaks me out to have giant bugs FLYING AT MY FACE. Suppressing my natural urge to flail my arms wildly was not easy.

I was not happy to experience the St. Louis Carousel at the Butterfly House with 60 hand carved horses and four deer. It's located in a corporate-looking, single-story box of a building on the Butterfly House grounds. The inside is a surprisingly dark room, empty except for the carousel and ticket seller. It's almost creepy. And the loud calliope music echoing off the empty walls doesn't make it any less creepy. The carousel could have been amazing. It's an original 1920s carousel from the Dentzel Co. of Philadelphia. It was installed, according to the brochure, at the St. Louis Highlands Amusement Park in 1929.

Butterflies (misunderstood) pouring out (misinterpreted). Some of the kids stopped grabbing at the butterflies and started to look a little worried. One inquisitive student had a question her teacher couldn't answer—they called over a worker, a degreed entomologist. They have a staff entomologist? He beamed with knowledge; everyone was beaming. You never know what you'll witness at the butterfly station. I saw a butterfly emerge from a chrysalis right before my eyes. It was a wonder: a wonder where wonder takes flight!

THE GRRRREAT HISTORY of that

urban   housing   disaster

P R U I T T - I G O E !

(The Wendell O. Pruitt Homes and William Igoe Apartments

known as Pruitt-Igoe)

The most genteel part of this story is the namesakes: Wendell O. Pruitt and William Igoe are not household names, nor even well-known St. Louisans such as Josephine Baker, Maya Angelou, Chuck Berry, or William S. Burroughs. Pruitt and Igoe are known primarily for their association with the infamous Pruitt-Igoe housing project. They were chosen, in part, because the proposed units were to be segregated: the Wendell Pruitt homes (for Black residents, named after a heroic Black WWII military pilot) and the William Igoe apartments (for white residents, named after an Irish-American Congressman). This segregated proposal was deemed illegal by the time construction actually began on the projects, but the name stayed on.

Many would describe Pruitt-Igoe as the greatest disaster in postwar public housing. After WWII, the vast population of Black St. Louisans was zoned into the most depleted and uninhabitable areas of St. Louis, especially the northside. By the early 1950s, the municipal eyes of the city were looking towards tearing down the decayed northside and building an expansive housing project. Pruitt-Igoe was rolled out to be a modernist wonder: designed by Minoru Yamasaki (later of World Trade Center fame), 33 eleven-story units, complete with playgrounds, gardens, and modern amenities. Yamasaki adhered to many of Le Corbusier's planning principles, but, due to the Korean War, the budget for building supplies had to be modified, and cheaper materials were used. Still, Pruitt-Igoe was in the national spotlight. Architectural Forum praised it as: "the best high apartment of the year . . . utopic."

Pruitt-Igoe, however, is famous neither for its Modernist design nor its contribution to urban renewal, but, instead, is an icon for a disastrous housing project failure. By the end of the 1960s, Pruitt-Igoe was infamous for its crime, gang violence, drug dealing, and general decay. There are many reasons that point to the failure of this expansive housing project, but nearly all of them include the lack of government funds to maintain the buildings. Dysfunctions in heating, elevators, garbage disposal, rodent control, are just a few of the failures that residents had to endure. The plumbing pipes were weather-broken or frozen and, often, raw sewage appeared in the hallways. The compactors were perpetually broken, so the garbage piled up in the common areas. By the late 1960s, most of the units had missing windows in the dead of winter. As one former resident put it: "it's just unbelievable that they would spend the money to build these things but not the money to maintain them."

In addition to the failed infrastructure, Pruitt-Igoe residents had to endure humiliating regulations imposed by the Missouri Welfare Department. Most infamous was the "man in the house rules," which prohibited women who received Aid to Dependent Children (ADC) from living with men. At this time, the Missouri Welfare Department barred many fathers not just from living with their families, but from legally living in the state of Missouri! Women in Pruitt-Igoe were not allowed to have men in their apartments and receive ADC due to their perceived reproductive irresponsibility. Policymakers assumed that if men were in the home, poor women on welfare would inevitably have more children and cost taxpayers more money. So by 1959, women headed the majority of households in Pruitt-Igoe.

Also, this particular Pruitt-Igoe welfare office performed periodic visits to individual apartments to monitor women's actions. Women's apartments became public spaces where the state intervened in and regulated the lives of women and their children. One resident, Quincie, recalled how representatives from the welfare office visited the family's apartment:

We were visited to check on standards for cleanliness!

The walls always had to be painted white. The welfare office restricted the type of food we bought, the jobs we could apply for—surveillance was a constant fixture.

And then it all came crashing down, literally. In 1972, less than twenty years after it was erected, Pruitt-Igoe began to be demolished.

That April, the demolition of two towers was aired live on TV news and attracted great public interest around the world as a symbol of urban renewal gone wrong. Postmodern architectural historian Charles Jencks called this destruction "the day Modern architecture died." As an aside, it is a strange coincidence that these two Yamasaki designs—Pruitt-Igoe and the World Trade Center—were both exploded, toppled, and viewed on TV around the world. Since its demolition, more hidden information has surfaced about Pruitt-Igoe. In the mid 1950s, in order to test the geographic range of chemical or biological weapons, the US Army Chemical Corps sprayed zinc cadmium sulfide via blowers onto the roofs of the Pruitt-Igoe buildings and at the nearby public schools. This was known as operation Large Area Coverage (or LAC, ironically).

At the time, local officials were told that the government was testing a smoke screen that could shield St. Louis from aerial observation in case the Russians attacked. But in 1994, the government admitted the tests were part of a biological weapons program and St. Louis was chosen because it bore some resemblance to the Russian cities that the US might attack.

One former resident of Pruitt-Igoe, Doris, was a baby in 1955, when her father died inexplicably. She recalled a summer day playing baseball with other kids in the street when a squadron of green Army planes flew close to the ground and dropped a powdery substance. She went inside, washed the dusty film off her face and arms, then went back out to play. She watched four siblings die of cancer, and battled four types of cancer herself—breast, thyroid, skin, and uterine.

II.

Who doesn't have something
to say about repetition? During
the Christmas season of 1975,
I was hired by Hickory Farms
at Frontenac Mall for the holiday rush:

                              the cry of the wolves (which turn
out to be the manager's dachshunds), my unreasonable
dread of the giant cheese slicer in the cooler,
operating like an oversized paper cutter—

                                     its thin wire blade,
like a piano string, pulled down onto a great wheel
of Gruyère,

                              the upbeat cheer of the holiday
gift baskets, shrink-wrapped, separated from the fancier
crumbling blue cheeses and the awe
of imported jams and preserves—at the entrance,
free samples of German sausage slices.

I was considered a hard worker and was
kept on after the holidays, even promoted
and given a largely insignificant title.

Before my Saturday shift, sometimes I'd attend
ballet classes at the Creve Coeur Dance Academy

located in a dingy strip mall of one-story structures:
Hacker's Barbershop, Raise-A-Racquet, Sherman
Bros Deli, Bagel Factory, Krummenacher Drugs,
and China Taste as the caboose.
Yes, ballet! and truth be told, it was odd for me.

Zero

        talent for it! But I was curious
about Modern Dance and being contrary was a plus—
besides, someone told me

to do ballet first, like the wisdom of advising
a teen to learn classical guitar before rock.
The dance studio was one room, brightly lit,
with two walls of mirrors. The front window faced
the parking lot so that onlookers could peer in.
I was always on the lookout: less embarrassed by my tights
than by my balance, which was troubling.
I was, by far, the worst in the class. The only other guy
was excellent and limber and spoke French.

        Ah, français, as in *Creve Coeur*!

   I was no Nureyev, nor erudite, nor Erasmus
   but my high school, Parkway North,
   Home of the Vikings, had an *outstanding*
   state-of-the-art theater and dance program.
   In Modern Dance, I was an equally clumsy dancer but . . .

I shined

   as a choreographer! Or at least I could mimic
   a Merce Cunningham performance I recently saw.

            And this is where
the trouble began. My dance teacher, first name Lorilee,
recommended me for a pre-college
Modern Dance masterclass at Washington University.
I was awarded the scholarship and figured my parents
would be proud, at least for the part about free tuition.

     The class met on ten consecutive Saturdays
which would mean quitting my Hickory Farms
job and walking away from that
           tempting promotion.
But my parents took no pride in this dance business
and were less than pleased about the whole ordeal.

They had their own worries: my dad's job
at the department store, demoted since he hadn't agreed
to relocate, my mom's daily nursing home visits
to feed lunch to her mother who was in a vegetative state,
and my aunt, sickly and envious, who would wind up
in the hospital if we got new furniture,

         my brother's volatile
episodes, my other brother's Vietnam draft
lottery number (not favorable), the front yard
zoysia grass experiment which would unpredictably
die and then revive sporadically . . .

Cheddar and sausage log gift packs versus leotards,
I figured, would be of little consequence.
But when an article about me appeared in the local paper,
my parents went into an invasion-of-privacy fit.

In that same *Jewish Light*,
an article about a Creve Coeur man
who, after his mother died, was shocked to discover a box
in her freezer that contained not a wedding cake,
as he'd always been told, but the mummified remains
of a newborn baby, wrapped in a pink blanket,

skin and hair intact after three decades.
Mr. Cooper said he freaked out and immediately
called the police! *I'm finding out my mom wasn't*

who I thought she was!

Mr. Cooper told *Jewish Light* that she never told him
what was in that box, not even on her deathbed.
Police have described the situation as *delicate—*
they are treating the discovery as a suspicious death.

Clearly!
Mr. Cooper just wants to know who the baby is. *Clearly!*
Clearly!

He said questions about what was in the box
were always off limits.
The box had been in her freezer for as long as
he could remember. They were silent about it.
Cooper explained that his mother had always
been secretive by nature, sometimes
disappearing for weeks. He suggested that his mother
may have been responsible for the baby's death,
adding that he's confused and angry.

This is what

America is all about right now, ask anyone.
Most St. Louisans, or at least the people I know
in Creve Coeur, are just trying to distract themselves
with *Dungeons* or the gym.

          On a log, Ms. Sophia M. Sachs
in front of her Butterfly House! Somebody
had to stage that *St. Louis Jewish Light* photograph.
And somebody has to landscape the bushes
along the walkway to the Butterfly House
and somebody has to count and recount the money
in the gift shop cash register.

          Somebody, certainly *not* Ms. Sachs,
has to clean the Butterfly House long after
the school kids are gone, and somebody
on a tractor, with headphones,

                    in the miserable heat,

has to mow the grass at the sprawling Monsanto campus.
Somebody at the Drury Inn and Suites

                    after a blowout high school

                          reunion party
has to clean the rooms and change the sheets and towels.
Somebody at Platinum Hair Salon in the Heritage Place
Mall has to shampoo hair and massage around
30 scalps a day.

Somebody at the Walgreens on Olive and Graeser
has to manage an angry customer, accusing her
of changing policies while she's trying to fill
a prescription by counting the pills
with a medical spatula on a metal tray.

Somebody has to stay late
in the teachers' lounge at Pattonville High
to discuss a plagiarized student composition
about future goals. Somebody in the kitchen
of La Bonne Bouchée, likely the dishwasher,

has to scrape off the crusted Swiss cheese from
the French onion soup crocks. At the Creve Coeur
Counseling Associates, somebody has to counsel
the teenager who refuses to eat and somebody,
often the same person, has to counsel the parents.

Somebody at De Smet Jesuit High School had to inflate
the basketballs during their improbable undefeated
32–0 season led by Steve Stipanovich, later of NBA fame.
Somebody had to write the feature story of the "Stipo" scandal
which is largely forgotten today.

Apparently, he accidentally shot himself

with a firearm in the shoulder.
He initially told police that a masked intruder,
wearing cowboy boots and a flannel shirt,
broke into his apartment and shot him while
screaming obscenities about basketball players.

The next day, Stipanovich recanted the story
and admitted that he shot himself by accident.
Years later, Stipo said: *That gun incident changed my life.*

Absolutely. It was in the past, and I had to look to the future.
I mean, you can't unscramble eggs . . .

                                   It was one of those
brutally cold snowy mornings and we were standing outside
under a tent for Uncle Leo's funeral service—
it was getting really long. I kept glancing over
at two cemetery workers behind the gravesite,
leaning on their shovels, wool overcoats, patient.
As is the tradition, we all tossed a shovel full
of dirt onto the coffin and then the workers
took over and finished the job.

                                  Everybody started the slow walk
back to their cars parked randomly around the cemetery.
There was some talk about going directly to the house
to sit shiva, but the immediate family needed some time.
So we went to TGI Fridays (now just Fridays,
having dropped the confusing *Thank God It's*)
in the Westgate Mall.

> The Grand Opening plastic flags blowing
> cheerfully, our buy-one-entree-get-one-free
> coupon, the peppermint striped awning—
> all felt like mockery after a funeral.
>
>   My dad got the steak
> and asked for the whiskey glaze on the side.
> It came with the whiskey glaze on top, of course.
>
>   We anticipated a fuss,
> but after a weighty pause, he approved
> while pushing the sauce around with his knife.
> The stained-glass lighting appeared

                    dim for a family restaurant.
The bar/hostess area was blaring Gary Stewart's
I've got this drinkin' thing, to keep from thinkin' things . . .
it didn't help at all.

Our table was sticky, too,
which reminded me of the whiskey glaze.

         A few minutes later,
my Wednesday Burger arrived. I ordered it medium rare
and let's just leave it at that. The table next to us
was enjoying an oversized basket of nachos.
They looked pretty good. We talked about family in Memphis
and how hot it is there, how Uncle Leo called mom *flea*
and how she enjoyed whatever

                    little attention she got.

I suggested we try the nachos next time.
Mom and dad looked like some horrible news
had just been delivered. Sorry I even mentioned
the nachos,

                    and The Blue Raspberry Lemonade
was tempting no one at our table.
and it's a lonely thing . . .
but it's the only thing . . .

           The power walker, headphones on,
sings along and reflects upon all of the wonderful life
choices he has made. He feels fortunate
as he smiles to himself and quickens his pace.
His arms swing with pride. And, like the song says,
he's thinking of that Creve Coeur love suicide,
the Falls, the Memorial Park, and the bird's-eye

view of the broken-hearted crack at the mouth
of the lake.

What is it about the calm of the walking trail,
so special from other silences? Other desires?
A whole neighborhood's desires? *Here's a plan*,
the power walker calculates: *Essen Hardware*

*is about a mile away which is around the corner
from Schnucks which works with my daily route.*
He runs through his list of chores for the week:
*number one is to take care of those weeds and pick up
some Roundup.* But he does feel a bit uneasy
about this morning's article in the *St. Louis Post-Dispatch*
on Monsanto's cancer lawsuits and the Bayer Corporation

buyout and how Bayer is paying $10 *billion*—
he emphasizes to himself—to settle Roundup lawsuits.
Just recently there were 25,000 lawsuits
against Monsanto, and they settled almost 100,000.
The article goes on to state that the average payout
for an individual who has been diagnosed

with non-Hodgkin's lymphoma is between
$5,000 and $25,000. *But obviously,* he reminds himself,
*Roundup, wouldn't still be on the shelves if . . .
anyway, the* St. Louis Post-Dispatch *always
sensationalizes to increase sales,* he shakes his head.

He has tried other products, but nothing compares.
In fact, the power walker recalls, *I tried several products
with very positive reviews, but the weeds
would only get sick, they wouldn't die.*

*I'll stick with Roundup until someone
can come up with an equally effective product.*

Does he feel edgy?—the natural
swinging motion of his arms feels heavy.
Does he think back to that windy day when he was spraying
Roundup and accidentally sprayed some areas
that he didn't want dead, and had to replace a lot of grass?

The long rhythm of my strides, he boasts
to himself, *would impress anyone! Even my neighbor Tom!
Objectively speaking, Tom has a better yard, no doubt,
but one moment's envy is the next moment's inspiration.
I'll get there,* he tells himself, *probably next year.*

Get poisoned or get on board. That's the choice that Monsanto is forcing upon soybean farmers in the Midwest. The past few summers, the farmers near Joe Brzocek's farm in central Missouri sprayed so much of the weed killer dicamba that it polluted the air for hours and sometimes days. As Brzocek puts it, there are two types of soybeans: Monsanto's, which are genetically engineered to withstand dicamba, and everyone else's.

Brzocek's soybeans are the damaged ones. His soybean leaves curl up, and the plants become smaller and weaker. He's lost as much as 40 bushels an acre in some fields, a huge loss when organic soybeans are $20 a bushel. He has to hold his breath every year to see if the damage will cause him to lose his organic certification.

His neighbors who spray dicamba are frustrated with him, he says. There's an easy solution to avoid damage, they tell him: buy Monsanto's seeds. This reality is what Monsanto was counting on when it launched dicamba-tolerant crops. Monsanto's new system was supposed to be the future of farming, providing farmers with a suite of seeds and chemicals that could combat more and more weeds that were becoming harder to kill. Instead, the system's rollout has led to millions of acres of crop damage across the Midwest and South; widespread tree death in many rural communities, state parks, and nature preserves; and an unprecedented level of strife in the farming world.

Executives from Monsanto and BASF, a German chemical company that worked with Monsanto to launch the system, knew their dicamba weed killers would cause large-scale damage to fields across the United States but decided to push them on unsuspecting farmers anyway, in a bid to corner the soybean and cotton markets. Monsanto and BASF have denied for years that dicamba is responsible for damage, blaming farmers

making illegal applications, weather events, and disease. The companies insist that
when applied according to the label, dicamba stays on target and is an effective tool
for farmers. Monsanto released seeds resistant to dicamba in 2015 and 2016 without
an accompanying weed killer, knowing that off-label spraying of dicamba, which is
illegal, would be "rampant." At the same time, BASF ramped up production of illegal
older versions of dicamba to apply to the crops and made tens of millions of dollars
selling the older versions. Monsanto and BASF knew about dicamba's propensity
to harm farmers' livelihoods and the environment before releasing the weed killer.

> *They fail. They limp with corns. I*
> *think he means to kill me, I don't know*
> *what to do. He comes in after midnight,*
> *I pretend to be asleep. He stands there,*
> *I feel him looking down at me, I*
> *am afraid.*

                Who? Was there any grand ribbon-
cutting ceremony when Bayer bought Monsanto?

Who? *Bayer Corporation, Bayer aspirin!*
The disastrous economic impact on farmers . . . Who?
Farmers! The face of the Falls grows impatient,
its outstretched arms encircling the woods . . . flailing . . .

When John Francis Queeny set up shop in St. Louis in 1901,
he named the company after his wife
Olga Méndez Monsanto.
The company was founded on one primary product:
saccharin, which was otherwise available only
from Germany. The operation took off
and soon expanded to other products:

caffeine, vanillin, aspirin, synthetic rubber, synthetic fibers.

After World War II, Monsanto successfully
moved into herbicides, using Western-themed
brand names like Ramrod, Lasso, and Roundup.
Edgar Queeny, the son of the founder,
took over in 1928. He was, ironically,
a noted conservationist. His book *Prairie Wings*
was called a "classic study of American wildfowl in flight."
Edgar co-produced several Nature documentaries,
including some in Africa, in cooperation
with the famous Kenyan guide Donald Ker.

Ok, stop right there! From my perspective I'm not arguing with you, I'm simply trying to explain that our store location doesn't carry that many sizes. No, I'm not stoned or drunk. Are you trying to get me fired or what!

A brief story: My mom worked for Studio Branca, very near Mason and Olive though I can't picture the exact coordinates as the boxes have shifted since—to the left of Dierbergs? same strip mall as Pastries of Denmark? —and I'd have to go to work with her all the time as a child.

It surprises me in hindsight that she was allowed to do this—bring a 6-year-old kid into a spa setting where women are trying to relax—but there we were. And I'd just learned the word "uptight" and something about it really tickled me, perhaps because it was one of the first compound words I'd really thought about or thought bizarre-sounding, nonsensical. So I sat in a vacant hair-cutting chair, spinning 'round, pumping myself up and down, while women would get their hair cut and colored and blown out. They'd offer niceties, I'd listen to their life a little bit, then hit 'em with: "Oh, you're just uptight." That day was the last they ever let me back in. Calling a white suburbanite uptight is basically the closest thing we have to a slur, I guess. My mom nearly lost her job over it!

You know who never lost their job, though? My extremely racist stepdad who has nosed his way into sergeant on the Ballwin police force after twenty+ years there. He used to begrudgingly take me to St. Monica's Elementary School as he listened to either the Bob and Tom show OR he had these CDs with songs about racist jokes. This is what pumped through my ears on the way to Catholic school.

Thanksgiving dinner with my mom's side was always like a smear campaign, like shooting lox in a brunchy barrel. She lives all the way out in Pacific, MO now, out past Six Flags, but we don't talk much anymore. If you think Creve Coeur is bad, the malintent out there is so thick you could slice it with a steak knife. In all of West County, the history is probably uglier but the camouflage is better. Growing up in Creve Coeur, though, the question wasn't: "I wonder what happened here in the past of this place?" but . . . "hey, who's got the best swimming pool?" At the front of the subdivision I grew up in is a massive cemetery, which has changed corporate ownership so many times I'm not sure what it's called anymore. You know the one, on Mason. I worked at a place called Hair Saloon for Men as a shoeshine boy, in between a cigar store and Lix—a pretty good custard shop, now long gone—attached to the Schnucks mall. My cousin, who would've been my age, has a memorial bench beside Creve Coeur Lake, apparently filled with the tears of that Osage woman (if memory serves, this is what the placard says . . . though if the eponymous conceit stayed true to itself, wouldn't that lake be pumped full of blood?). He died of a heroin overdose.

H.

III.

Ghosts? Oh man.
One thing I can tell you for sure is that I have
zero experience with hauntings. However,
I'd be remiss not to mention the ghost
of the Creve Coeur Falls—locals swear
they've seen the ghost of the woman who supposedly
leapt to her death from the Falls into the lake.
Apparently, there are consistent reports

spotting a figure leaping from the Falls
late at night and disappearing as she reaches
the lake's surface. Others report a moaning or
                              sobbing heard under the Falls.

Also, I should mention that
there's another explanation altogether
different about the Creve Coeur namesake

but it's hardly ever mentioned and
it has no lover's suicide and it's a lot
less *Pocahontas*:

Michel Guillaume Jean de Crèvecœur
served in the French and Indian War
as a cartographer. After the war, in 1759,
he moved to New York, adopted the English-American

name of John Hector St. John, and in 1770 married
Mehitable Tippet, the daughter of a New York merchant.

He prospered as a farmer and started writing about life
in the American colonies. He was the first popular author
to introduce Europeans to the melting pot idea:

this New American . . . who is either a European,
or the descendant of a European, hence that strange mixture
of blood, which you will find in no other country.

Here's another myth: *By 1950, St. Louis City*
had reached its peak population, forcing returning soldiers
to look for housing in St. Louis County.

Wage-earners wanted bigger houses, more yard space,
and places to park their new cars. The automobile industry
had a vision of two cars for every suburban family:

one for dad to go to work, and one for mom
to drive to the market or to the kids' activities.
The new affordability

in the automobile industry, along with
the construction of highways, further pushed
the westward movement away from downtown.

> Put that expansion-to-the-suburbs myth
>   next to the real Harland Bartholomew,
> urban planner, whose vision was
>   renovation by demolition.
>
> For Bartholomew, the bulldozer
>   was the best tool for postwar

urban planning. His vision guaranteed
no people of color could participate
   in this westward movement

to the suburbs. In 1939,
   St. Louis approved his proposal
to demolish more than twenty square miles
   of inner-city real estate,

more than 400 apartment buildings
   and houses, mostly renters, mostly
Black families. And with the destruction
   of those homes, came the destruction

of a bohemian culture
   of bookstores and coffeehouses,
demolishing what was once
   termed the Greenwich Village

of the West. To this day,
   massive stretches of downtown
St. Louis remain
   either scorched or poorly

developed—handfuls of low-rise buildings
   stand alone on empty lots and
stretches of highway on-ramps
   headed west to the suburbs.

Everybody has roots.

We go on living. We permit ourselves,
Mr. Paterson, *to continue.*
For whom? For who wants to hear it?

What is the story, the myth again, the namesake?
Tell it, please. Can it be told with pictures?
Through the State Historical Society of Missouri?

Their archives? County libraries? Court documents?
Can the story be told through transcripts,
revised transcripts, revised interpretations?

Something else, something else the same.

   I have to say that for our event, my husband was very anxious about the banquet hall. He was more concerned about covering those ugly banquet chairs than he was about the actual event itself. But we found an outstanding company that covers chairs for exactly occasions like ours—my in-laws' 50th wedding anniversary party. We Got You Covered! specializes in chair covers that go over those gross banquet chairs. It made a huge difference! My husband picked them out and they were beautiful! They were gold and white satin striped with gold lamé bows. And the funny thing about all of this is that I went to high school with the owner, Kathy. She was always doing arts and crafts, so it didn't surprise me when I learned that she started the chair covering business. She told me that the business really got started because of her own wedding! She liked the venue for her wedding but hated the banquet chairs, so she made her own covers and the rest is history.

I reflected on the ingratitude of the whites, when I saw their fine houses, rich harvests, and everything desirable around them; and recollected that all this land had been ours. 1833 memoir, Black Hawk, the great Sauk leader; later, as a prisoner, paraded around the Eastern cities as a curiosity.

Which Roundup Product Is Right For Me?

Roundup Ready-To-Use Weed & Grass Killer.
Roundup Mass Control 365.
Roundup Extended Control Weed & Grass Killer.
Roundup Poison Ivy Plus Tough Brush Killer.

Roundup Weed & Grass Concentrate Plus.
Roundup for Lawn Products (Northern & Southern Formulas).
Roundup for Lawns & Crabgrass Destroyer.
And which applicator is right for me?
Comfort Wand?—This wand is true to its name.
With one-touch continuous spray, it makes hand fatigue
a thing of the past. *Pump N Go 2 Sprayer?*—This sprayer
will give you up to ten minutes of continuous spray.
Trigger Sprayer?—Once a classic, always a classic.
This sprayer is all about great value and ease of use.
Each squeeze treats one weed.
Recommended Usage Areas: Driveways, Patios & Gravel,
Tress Rings and Mulch Beds, Vegetable Gardens,
Poison Ivy and Woody Brush, Fence Lines & Foundations.
Just remember, don't treat any plants you want to keep.

When Shirley Gold, who has born in downtown St. Louis and died in Creve Coeur, knew it was time to move into Brookdale Senior Living, she asked her kids help her with a Garage Sale. All paperback books were 25¢, hard covers $1. Toys, puzzles, and games up to $3. All jeans, including her husband Leon's, who had passed two years earlier, were $3. Purses were $5-10. Her daughter-in-law thought that price was especially low, but Shirley reminded her that none of them were expensive to start with, and she had already set aside the two purses for everyday use. Cassettes and CDs were all $1. Leon had a penchant for Original Film Soundtracks and Classical Music. The kitchen table was $25 and another $15 for the chairs. Shirley had strong feelings about the kitchen table—lots of memories—but she knew it was too big for her Brookdale one bedroom, and she had already picked out a smaller new one with her son Don who was going to pick it up himself the next week. She priced all of the shoes at $1-3, which did give Shirley some pause because she often treated herself to finely made shoes, but she never wore them anymore and they were just collecting dust in the closet.

No one is asking you to *not* learn more
about Elton John's *Philadelphia Freedom*
but I just want to express my own freedom
by suggesting that this song, like so many pop songs,
can mean a lot of different things to different listeners.
I'm not from Philly, I'm from St. Louis County,

Elton isn't from Philly either, so I don't think the song
is about the place, but it's true that any song
named for a place is bigger than just one place.
Philadelphia Freedom can be a patriotic song,
and a gay rights song, *and* a song about
Billie Jean King's World Tennis Team.
When I'm driving down Olive Blvd. and I'm listening
to Elton's classic song, am I thinking about Billie Jean King's
World Tennis Team and gay rights?

                Hell no! But as my friend (another
huge Elton fan) points out—it's hard to argue
against the Billie Jean King connection
because the original vinyl record label reads:
to BJK and the sound of Philadelphia.

   Don't get me wrong. I do hear what you're saying about the tennis connection, the '70s gay rights movement, the Philadelphia sound, all of it. I feel democratic about embracing all of the possible analyses and that's where my American freedom comes in, if you will! So, hey, I will support you if you want to make a gay liberation interpretation of these lines: "You can live your life alone . . . some people choose the city . . . some others choose the good-old family home . . . I like living easy without family ties . . ." But, to be honest, at that time, around 1975, everyone was flooded with bicentennial crap. Elton and Bernie might have had that in mind, too, when they were writing this song, but I doubt it seeing that they're Brits. I'm not gonna make any claims about it. Maybe they were getting into the whole spirit of the thing. Maybe it was an exploited coincidence. The timing might be a year or so off, but as I remember it there was a sort of vague patriotism even among rockers and rebels. The little bit of resistance I saw to all of the bicentennial consumption was more in the form of an eye roll, or an anti-bicentennial T-shirt. Products were everywhere. American businesses were marketing the bicentennial by reinforcing the notion that commerce and economic consumption were part of who we are as Americans . . . you know, our identity. In celebration of America's 200th birthday, McDonald's had red, white, and blue milkshakes, Zippo designed an American flag lighter, and Poulan sold a bicentennial special limited edition Poulan 76 chainsaw in red, white, and blue. Commemorative kitsch was especially big in housewares: plates, mugs, water pitchers, and glasses decaled with an eagle, or the likeness of George Washington, or John Adams, or the American flag, or Archibald Willard's familiar Revolutionary fife and drum trio. I remember the Pepsi bicentennial campaign was especially cloying with that apostrophe in their "feelin' free" logo. I remember picking up some American flag rolling papers—not sure if it was patriotic or rebellious to watch one's joint burn in red, white, and blue. Even the US Government got into the act with minting special commemorative bicentennial quarters and silver dollars. It was like consumption took hold as the centerpiece for American patriotism. Buying kitschy products was considered an act of economic (anti-British) independence. *Philadelphia Freedom* doesn't exactly fit that sentiment.

In 2012, I met Billie Jean King. I had just gotten a coupon for Outback Steakhouse, so I asked her if she wanted a blooming onion. She said no, but she flashed that winning smile. I didn't ask for an autograph because I've never asked anyone ever for an autograph. I felt a little awkward not asking for the autograph which seems like the normal thing to do, like she was sort of expecting it . . . certainly instead of the blooming onion coupon. On the ride home, I was humming *Philadelphia Freedom*—I think it's written to her—and I had wished afterward that I would have asked her about that. Rumor has it that Elton and Billie met at a party, that they became fast friends, that Billie had a custom tracksuit made for Elton (yes!), and that Elton's form of thanks was to write her a hit song.

'76 was the same year
I worked as a Sea Hatch busboy—an upscale
seafood restaurant in land-locked Westgate Plaza:
half shopping mall, half corporate park.
The menu read: *Spawned in the fresh*
clear waters of the oceans of the world
and then tenderly harvested and air freighted
to our doors . . .
If you look about we think you will notice

how management combed the world, literally,
to acquire many of our accoutrements.
For example, our dining tables are all ship hatches
recovered from sunken vessels in the Caribbean,

brought to St. Louis, sand-blasted,
and then treated with a special epoxy to expose
the magnificent oak graining.

Sometimes after my Sea Hatch shift ended, my brother would pick me up and take me downtown to Herbie's. In the 70s, Herbie's was *the* gay disco in St. Louis. My brother would sneak me in and we'd hurry upstairs to the dance floor. For $5 you could buy a small bottle of amyl nitrite, poppers, from the DJ. Everybody had poppers. The dance floor swayed like a fish tank. One night, there was a police raid and the DJ cut off Donna Summer's *Love To Love You Baby* to announce: "everyone underage get out!" No one left; everyone started digging through pockets for their Herbie's membership cards. After that night, Herbie's become stricter and had a doorman. The next time I went there, I was refused entry and my brother had to call me a taxi to go home—a taxi in Creve Coeur? What a scandal! A few years later, two of the managers at Herbie's died of AIDS, and they closed down shortly after. And a few years after that, my brother also died of AIDS.

    Is there a right way to power walk?

    Any movement, no matter what you do,
    is better than none. But if you want to get faster
    and fitter, then it does make sense to pay attention
    to your walking form.

    There's plenty to think about
    from head to toe: how your feet
    hit the ground, the movement
    of your hips, the angle you lean,
    the swing of your arms,
    even the direction of your gaze.

    Don't look down at your feet. It slows you down.
    Instead, stand tall, keep your chin level to the ground,
    your shoulders back, your chest lifted, your abs tight.

    You wouldn't run with your arms straight at your sides—
    it would slow you down. Same goes for walking. Like a pendulum,
    the shorter your arm is, the faster it swings. And because our bodies
    like to be in sync, your legs will speed up to stay in tune with your arms.

As your leg swings forward, your heel should be
the first part of your foot to hit the pavement.
Focus on keeping those toes up as you land. Then roll
from your heel to your toes as smoothly as possible.
Finally, push off with your toes to propel forward.
After you roll from your heel to your toes, focus on really
pushing off the ground to propel yourself forward.
For maximum power, bend at the ball of your foot, raising
the back of your foot as if you were trying to show the person
behind you the sole of your shoe.

> Shorter, quicker steps are the key to going faster.
> Don't make the mistake of overstriding.

> Too many walkers reach their front leg out farther than normal.
> Instead of speeding you along, these big steps actually
> slow you down because it's harder to get your balance right.

#1: So, you're telling me all of this technique for what?
I'm interested in the final results.

#2: Let me belabor the obvious: done poorly, you *will* sustain
injury and is your body not your temple?

In a sense, your leg acts as a break. When you take steps
that are too long, you have a choppy stride and you actually
increase the impact of each step, which, in turn, may boost
your risk for injury. Shorter, quicker steps allow for a smooth,
rolling stride, and they make it easier for you to shift your body
weight over your front leg and swing your back leg forward.

                         The result:
a faster walking speed. And don't let me stop you if you want
to add some power to your arm swing. Imagine that your back
                                   muscles are pulling

your arms back. Squeeze your shoulder blades
and drive your elbows behind you, keeping them close
to your body.

Then let one arm swing naturally forward as you pull
the other one back so the work is on the back swing.
Remember to keep your shoulders down and relaxed,
not pulled up toward your ears. Trust me, these techniques
will save your life!

Like with so many other aspects of our daily lives,
power walking needs to take advantage of gravity.
Walking is actually a series of forward falls,
and we catch ourselves with our front leg.

                                            Don't make the common
mistake of resisting gravity. Instead,
lean into your walk a little bit, about five degrees, and the lean
should come from your ankles. Don't bend at your waist.
To get a feel for this, try it while standing still.

Don't worry if it feels clumsy at first.
You'll get used to it. Just remember:
it's all about anatomy, mathematics,
and physics (gravity). Trust yourself.

You can do this by standing comfortably
in front of a mirror at home.
Work on pulling your elbows back behind you,
so your hands swing back slightly behind your hips.
It might seem counterintuitive, but this backward
swing of the arm will help propel you forward faster.

        Think about this shift.

    The Metropolitan Sewer District is working to repair a significant water main break near Creve Coeur Lake Park. The break occurred in a force main, a pressurized pipe that carries water, sewage, and other materials. Raw sewage spilled onto the road and into drainage ditches near the pumping station on Creve Coeur Mill Road. Signs were posted on the walking and bike paths in the park.

                              The whole area goes hush
when flooding gets mentioned—
not just the walkers and the runners

                              but the memory, for everyone,
of the several hundred-thousand gallons sewage spill
still looms large. Nobody will know the total damage
until the clean-up and repairs are complete.
But when folks hear the word *flooding* around here

                              they think of the Mississippi River
and the very real sandbags along the bank, and then
the collective trauma around flooding, even the word itself,
gets applied to these lesser spillage situations,
                              and the County Parks Department
blocks off the walking paths around Creve Coeur Lake.

The parks department went on the news to remind West County
citizens that this is a sewage spill contained around Creve Coeur Lake,
not a river flooding   .   .   .   .   .

N.B. "In 1782, a French immigrant, Hector St. John de Crèvecoeur, published *Letters from an American Farmer*, an influential meditation on what it means to become an American. In his letters, Crèvecoeur portrays America as a magical place of the encrusted beliefs, customs, and traditions that had disfigured European society. Here a new race of men had emerged. The book became the first literary success by an American author in Europe and turned Crèvecœur into a celebrated figure. He was the first writer to describe to Europeans the life on the American frontier and to explore the concept of the American Dream, portraying American society as characterized by the principles of equal opportunity and self-determination. Crèvecoeur writes: 'What then is the American, this new man? Leaving behind him all ancient prejudices and manners, he receives new ones from the new mode of life he has embraced, the government he obeys, and the new rank he holds. He becomes an American by being received in the broad lap of our great Alma Mater. Here individuals of all nations are melted into a new race of men.'"

—*Letters from an American Farmer*, J. Hector St. John

BOOK TWO

(2020)

Sunday in Creve Coeur Memorial Park

___

I.

Outside
        of *Furious 7*
                the entire *Fast & Furious*
franchise is just so-so, the power walker contemplates
the opening
        scene carnage:
           two hospital workers huddled
behind an EKG machine—

        an armed SWAT team slain
        and scattered about the hospital
        hallways, elevators, lobby

—the sinister assassin casually walking away from the hospital,
 back turned to the grenade about to explode . . .

        BOOM! screeching away
      in his Jaguar F-Type Coupe R!

The power walker shakes off the difference between
here and there

                              and strides ahead with a dedicated pace
along the Creve Coeur Lake path.
It's the quietest place on earth. He hums the chorus
of a Doobie Brothers' tune to drown out the bloody *Furious* scene.

Some dogs bark.

                              No one cares

              about who you are, or who you say you are—
they care about belonging and they care about who
can accelerate that for them, and who can blame them
for wanting to feel like they belong and who . . .

                              Woof! Woof!

—the world is harsh
                    and the comforts
                                          are few!
A wildflower on my path! The walker is in tune.

American mink, river otter, yellow coneflower,
rose turtlehead, plains pocket gopher, red squirrel,
Bagel Factory, pied-billed grebe, woodland vole,
cooper's hawk, purple beardtongue,

                              The Global
Quesadilla Company, eastern cottontail, muskrat,
Il Bel Lago, southern bog lemming, The Hive,
Pasta House Co., pine warbler,
FroYo, blue lobelia, house sparrow.

Walking   —

>   hispid cotton rat, thirteen-lined ground squirrel,
>   lance leaf coreopsis (named Missouri Native Plant of the Year
>   for its outstanding qualities), Norway rat, big brown bat,
>   Lion's Choice,
>
>   Imo's Pizza, woodchuck, Panda Express,
>   Pastries of Denmark
>   Orzo Mediterranean
>   Grill
>   where is the path without rot?

Walking   —

The body is tilted slightly forward from the basic standing
position and the weight thrown on the ball of the foot,
while the other thigh is lifted and the leg and opposite
arm are swung forward (fig. 6B). Various muscles aided.

Walk with the Saint Louis Walkers in Bellefontaine Cemetery and Arboretum. Please join our yearly cemetery walk. How relevant to walk in a cemetery on Halloween, but, please, no costumes of any kind are allowed. This walk will be on a Sunday for the convenience of the cemetery. Well-behaved dogs are welcome (clean up, of course), but they are not allowed inside buildings. Register from 10 am-1 pm. We must finish by 4 pm. Cemetery gates are locked at 5 pm. Mark the date and times on your calendar. $3/walker.

  We have a new trail and a larger parking area with amenities. Two or three crypts will be open to view, with volunteers telling the stories. Bellefontaine is also a Level II Accredited Arboretum. Besides being a garden of beauty, inspiration, and historic significance, Bellefontaine has an accessible and diverse horticultural collection and has become an important natural sanctuary and habitat for wildlife in the urban environment. You can make a day of it! There is so much to see in this beautiful, peaceful place! This will be a very special walk—intermediate and advanced walkers are welcome! Interested in making a weekend out of it? Hurry and book your reservation at Drury Plaza Hotel, complimentary breakfast included with group code.

What is love—more than walking?

Walking gives you peace, solitude, and time to reflect.
Footsteps have a rhythm and a balance. Like a metronome,
they keep time for you. *It is the rhythm of life*, he concludes.

A former classmate asks me: *So, what do you do?*

This is at my 25th high school reunion, mind you.
I've been writing mostly.
Horses? . . .

A small cluster of alums gather around the snack chips—
it looks like things haven't gone so well, and behind them
there's another group, designer outfits, glowing.

   The Baby Tooth Survey was formed in 1958 by the Committee of Nuclear Information (CNI), a grassroots organization that included prominent scientists and citizens in St. Louis. The Tooth Survey collected hundreds of thousands of baby teeth from children born in the 1950s and 1960s in the St. Louis metropolitan area, using them to measure exposure to radiation from above-ground nuclear weapons tests conducted during the early years of the Cold War. The St. Louis's Baby Tooth Survey became a marvel of environmental activism, and its findings led to significant policy changes regarding nuclear weapons testing.

   After the Soviet Union's first successful nuclear weapons test in 1949, the United States kicked off a series of tests of its own. By 1958, dozens of above-ground tests had been conducted by the Americans, Soviets, and British, exposing humans the world over to dangerous nuclear fallout. An inaugural Atomic Energy Commission study, called "Project Sunshine" to deflect attention, measured the amount of radioactive particles in local cow's milk in 1955. St. Louisans grew alarmed when the US Public Health Service's 1956 report suggested that the St. Louis region was a "hot spot" for radioactivity. Concerned scientists and citizens founded the Committee for Nuclear Information (CNI) in March 1958 at a meeting organized by Edna Gellhorn, former president of the League of Women Voters in St. Louis.

The Baby Tooth Survey became the CNI's central project. In 1958, Johns Hopkins University biochemist Herman Kalckar had devised the ingenious idea in an article for the scientific journal *Nature*. Kalckar noted that the isotope strontium-90, a byproduct of nuclear fallout, followed the normal pathways of calcium and therefore collected in cow's milk, which children consumed while their deciduous teeth were forming. Hypothetically, if scientists could collect enough baby teeth, they could measure the uptake of Sr-90 in humans.

Through several years, the tests provided conclusive evidence for elevated levels of Sr-90 in children born during the years of above-ground nuclear weapons tests—a powerful proof of widespread exposure to radioactivity due to the nuclear arms race. The Baby Tooth Survey helped persuade President John F. Kennedy to negotiate a treaty with the Soviet Union to end above-ground testing of atomic bombs in 1963.

> *Your mind can go freely exploring like a melody.*
> He ponders. *For me it takes around twenty minutes for the rust*
> *and debris to slip from my mind, and then the air seems*
> *to reach the dusty corners and new thoughts emerge.*
> Green shoots grow. Oxygen moves around freely.

Walking —

> he leaves the path, finds it tough going
> but outstanding, across stubble and matted brambles:
> *walking,* he reflects, *helps develop my inner tenderness*
> *towards myself and towards the world around me.*
> *You refrain from making judgments*
>
> *too quickly,*
> because
>
> *when you are walking you have time*
>
> *to change your mind. This is the greatest*
> *freedom available: to be able to think without pressure.*
> *Walking allows space for speculation,*
> *space to experiment with thought and,*

most importantly, to not know the outcome
of that experiment. I've always been happy

                         with my own company, and walking
confirms the idea. Solitude unties me
from the distraction of other people's judgements.
When we learn to think for ourselves,
we feel our emotions with new clarity.

AND if I need to make a decision in my life,
I will always wait until I can go out walking
before I make it. I've never lost my preference for walking.
If I'm out with friends at night and someone

offers to drop me home, I nearly always turn them down.

I would much rather walk. I always take the long way home!
So if you need time to think, space to breathe,
room to save yourself, if you have some troubles
to sort out, go for a walk.

A teacher at Francis Howell High School was jogging
through the woods of Creve Coeur Park after work
when another man jumped out and opened fire on him.
The teacher took off sprinting
as the man continued to fire more rounds.

"What then?"

The next day, a man was apprehended
while hiding in those same woods.
Police say he'd been living in the woods

       for approximately two months.

    Inside his tent
                    were a few guns and about

                                      100 rounds of ammo.

    He also confessed to using a bow and arrow to kill a man.

SPARK! What is *Spark!*? *Spark!* provides high school students in the Parkway School District with dynamic, immersion-based student learning experiences to ensure students can respond to an ever-changing world. How did *Spark!* begin? Over the years we've seen students leave their four-year HS experience and struggle with the decisions they will face in terms of majors and life journeys—decisions that will impact their entire lives, with little to no real-world experience in an industry. *Spark!* directly interrupts and educates students at this level in an experiential way. This is why *Spark!* is such an important part of our school district. *Spark!* exemplifies how business, community and public education can partner to produce personalized learning experiences that educate the workforce of the future, especially in high skill, high demand jobs. The *Spark!* program is grounded in profession-based learning relying heavily on strong partnerships with business, industry, and post-secondary institutions. Emphasis is placed on developing professional and ethical skills which employers deem highly important to career success, such as: project management, time management, teamwork, and creativity, as well as empathy, communication, and community activism.

    In Autumn, the red and yellow leaves fool
    no one, not even the Falls,
    who calls out to the squirrels: *no one*

    is saying the circumstances make good impossible.
    A glossy brochure pictures a smiling couple

                  holding hands, a wavy blonde
    affluence, her bright print dress,
    his striped bell-bottoms, leaning against
    a stone wall—*when you are born you are soft*

and pliable, the stone breathes, the flesh does not
know what it does not want

to know.
It goes for a walk among
                        rocks, twigs, informational
signage in colorful Missouri Autumn!

The newlyweds on the brochure
                             combating waking
                             _____

                             hours unknown death
piecemeal.

Channel 4 News reports that police responded to a large disturbance at Parkway North High School Friday night. Police said they believe a gunshot was fired during one of many fights that broke out around the outside of the school. Students tell News 4 that several high schools were at the football stadium for a jamboree and teams were on the field when the alleged shots were fired. Witnesses said the panic started after someone yelled "he has a gun!" Police report that there were no serious injuries.

"Somebody pulled out their gun and then everybody started running because everybody got scared and didn't know what to do," said one student.

News 4 also interviewed several teachers: "You know the most unfortunate thing I see is a whole lot of kids with no parental supervision. We administrators and teachers and folks involved with afterschool activities are there for the enrichment of the students or we would not be there for the fifteen-hour days that it takes to hold these events."

The parents, according to News 4, are very upset about how this whole incident is being handled. One interviewed parent commented: "We have been in the district for years and have four children. People are talking. Please address what actually happened! People who were there are all over social media saying it was terrifying! The school and the police say the situation is "stable" but that's not a word I would use to describe it. And if there were no injuries then why were there ambulances all over the place?"

         A once proud Eads Bridge
         stretches across the muddy Mississippi—
         the very first US bridge constructed of steel.

Invention! . . . *unless there is a new mind* . . .
the Falls repeats each word: *invention,*
committee, policy, myth, massacre.
Yes, East St. Louis, just on the other side
of the Eads bridge. Who needs to hear my story?
The Falls shrugs: *desire, greed,* the view of the Falls
is wide but partial, seasonal, heartbroken, fickle . . .
a fur trapper story, a Jesse James hideout
(the overhang like an armpit),
an elementary school field trip gone wrong,
a ghost story, a story of joggers and walkers
and lovers above its head, an overdose story,
a park bench memorial plaque story,
a wink-to-the-future story, which is basically
a real-estate story, a Grand Opening balloon story
blowing over Schnucks . . . we were talking about
invention, a fleece zip-out lining for your overcoat.
The Falls sighs: *thunder—a profitable Spring line*.

Under a clump of bushes, two teenagers
are in love, they look up at the stars . . .
it's around midnight . . .

                            suddenly they stop.

—secrets that are not policies, books, an unlit park entrance—

> Four orbs cross the night sky
>   —one announces how fucked up he is
>   and slams the Bronco truck door.
> The sound of gravel twisting
> beneath their boots,
>
> upsetting the serenity of the lake.
> The lovers behind the bushes stay
> still . . .

one last stoned
guffaw wild in the distance . . .
the lovers exhale and return

to reciting a few lines from a book—
it helps if only to . . . *wait,
what was that?*

One of the lovers takes off their jacket—
a blanket over the moss
and dead leaves.

It's so still, can you hear?
It's almost silent. They move
their soft hands along their warm bodies

and struggle with each other's clothes.
A stillness rotating away from tenderness.
The eyes of the Falls are closed,

the folds in the limestone, more
the majestic wrinkles of an elephant than
the eroding steps of an ancient ruin.

Is haunting the thing that doesn't last?
The dreaded aura around the parked truck?
Where did they go this late?

*When is the park supposed to close anyway?
What's the best way back to Fee Fee Road?*
The sleepy Falls yawns and stretches

with a roar heard across the lake.
Turn on the weather channel! *Strange.
The flowers have no scent.*

The lovers scramble behind the bushes
to collect their things for the backpack:
a bottle of water, a book of poetry,

a baguette, some cheese still unwrapped,
a few cigarette butts
$\qquad\qquad\qquad$ in the weeds.

Walking   —

Creve Coeur's pioneer history is still evident in the Hackmann
and Clester cabins near Conway Park, the one-room

$\qquad$ Lake School House and the Tappmeyer
farmhouse, all built in the late 1800s. Many St. Louisans

$\qquad$ remember Creve Coeur as *the country* because it was
only incorporated in 1949, with just 1,900 residents.
It was a time when WWII veterans and their young families
wanted bigger houses and more yard space, and the newly
developed highways made downtown St. Louis accessible . . .

*Forget it! for God's sake, cut
out that stuff.*

Walking   —

A different day but the same trail, our power walker
takes great pleasure in the routine of his Sunday
exercise above the bluffs, looking down on the empty
gravel parking lot littered with cans of beer. *Nothing changes,*
he shakes his head, looks upward, disapprovingly.

                              Getting back to love, or more
            accurately, love lost, since everybody is singing about it,

            making up stories about the heartbroken

                leap from the Falls, about the adult
            who realizes the child in him is small
                                        and lost and not
                                                    sufficiently
            soothed or several other children who might
            have been killed recklessly

                                        no chance to contemplate

                                                    those feelings.
                Who's there?

                              On a stone bench by the lake, a young guy,
            maybe sixteen, strumming his guitar, and a bigger guy, with a beard thick
            for his age, is standing next to him singing along—a proud and gregarious
            baritone. The song is a duet about rejecting fatherly advice. Others in
            their group struggle along the edge of the lake: a few Imo's pizza boxes,
            Marlboros, Busch beer . . . it could almost be a picnic, except for that one
            dude, his name escapes me, wasted on quaaludes, flicking his cigarette into
            the void. *Balthazar!* That kid's name was Balthazar!

                              But everyone called him *Ballsy,*
                which, of course, he didn't like. I also heard him called *Belief*—
            his father was a Pastor—anyway I'm told he now runs
            a gunshop out of a Sunoco station in Rock Hill.

Dear H: We cannot ignore your honest letter and request to further discuss Provel cheese here. But there's a lot to explain if you're not from St. Louis. Firstly, let's be clear: it's disgusting and it's delicious. Even in our Gateway to the West city, few folks really know what Provel is, besides that it's smothered on pizzas and appears, mysteriously, like cheese worms, on many St. Louis salads at Italian restaurants. For starters, Provel is not even legally cheese. According to the FDA, Provel can't even be classified as cheese because it doesn't meet the requirements. So when I say "cheese," I'm really talking about Provel's official categorization: "pasteurized processed cheese."

Despite the popular myth that Provel is a combination of provolone and mozzarella, it's actually a mix of white cheddar, Swiss, and provolone cheeses (but doesn't taste like any of the three). With a low melting point and gooey texture, Provel is used on most of the pizza in St. Louis and when it cools down, it becomes a kind of plastic-y buttery substance.

"People from St. Louis love it," says the owner of Joe Fassi Sausage & Sandwich Factory on The Hill, the city's Italian neighborhood. "When we switched to provolone, people wanted the Provel." Others comment that Provel is a bit sharper: "Provel has more bite, more smokiness, more tang than, say, mozzarella," says a researcher at the St. Louis Central Library. It's a mysterious cheese my friend, no doubt.

       Actually, Creve Coeur Memorial Park is not
       in Creve Coeur but one town over in
       Maryland Heights.

                                        Actually,
       Creve Coeur proper only has a few small
       parks of its own, six to be accurate. I suppose
       the best one is Millennium Park,
       which is the largest.

       It features two unique playgrounds,
       and an outstanding splash pad operating
       with a push-button timer for each patrons' use
                              (only available in the summer months).

       Also, there's a soccer field, a softball field,
       and the historic Tappmeyer Homestead
       mentioned earlier.

                         Why is all of this
       necessary   for whom?   How could a city
                         be so barren?

The pocket gophers and the woodrats
enjoy some sun on the forehead of the Falls.
                    Their dreams? Seriously
aloof.

Let us be reasonable!

                    It isn't what you think it is,
a Sunday in Creve Coeur Park: the cry of
a red-tailed hawk, some commotion over who brought
what for the picnic, Frampton's *Show Me The Way*
with its talk box solo,
    lilting from a car radio . . .
                    and no one

to relate to 'cept the sea.

Stand downstream from the confluence
of the Missouri and Mississippi rivers and you'd be
near Earth City, now a giant corporate park
with over 400 businesses. It's built on flood lands
and secured by a 500-year levee. Once upon a time
the Little League ball fields were here
and one stormy Sunday, the sky turned a purplish beet
and a swirl of dirt kicked up from the infield,
like a string, to the darkening sky.

The parents started shouting for their kids
to hurry back to the cars—terrified, running
to the grassy parking lot in their baggy uniforms.
Of all days! A tornado threatening
                    on a Bar Mitzvah morning!
Standing inches away from the TV tracking the storm:
                    it was touch-and-go

for a minute there, but then the day went off without a hitch,

ending joyously with a party at The Flaming Pit banquet room
known in West County for their effortless catering.

                                      No one could get over
the creative appetizers. On the dance floor,

the parents take the first dance and feign happiness;
the teenagers shift about the circumference
studying each other's moves—the side step, the neck slide.
It's contagious. The Falls and the lake also slide in unison—
when no one is watching, the surface of the lake ripples,
the glittery teenagers do a bump, the caterers bob,
the dancing balloon above Schnucks sways in the wind.

                                      —Dear Creve Coeur Walkers!

It is essential to know what to bring:
water, broken-in hiking shoes over
tennis shoes, dress in layers (not sure what
the weather will do), a sun hat or a baseball cap
                         (preferably the Cards!),
small snacks—one or two protein bars—
remember, this is a hike not a picnic.

I met my ex-husband in a walking club.
Obviously it didn't work out, but if you're asking me
I'd say yes! it's a good place to meet people.
How to move on, though, is a good question—
you just do, you choose to.

                     You could choose to stay sad
and longing, or you could choose to move on. That's it.

The young guy who was playing the guitar
near the Falls had a quiet, deadpan voice.
The other, the big guy, wore a wide leather hat.

Did terror twist the wind? *Didn't notice.*

                                      The big guy
with the leather hat also had some moves.
                                        Is it here
or found
                anywhere in a book? *Nope.* Tell me,
where are you looking?

                We leap awake and what
                        we think we see fails us! Or worse,
what we actually see we seem not to see
and then

                something else fails us—remember
the other friends milling around the Imo's pizza boxes
by the edge of the lake and the built-in barbecue pit?

                                This is the year

we all got a little closer
to death.
        Blah!
                Gross!
                              Someone in the group
spits her pizza into a paper napkin. Everyone
looks on . . .

Remember that film where a woman is trying to escape
from a group of assassins, and she runs over

to the parked car of her former love interest
where the guy is sitting idly in the back seat?

                                        He stares at her
        blankly, pistol in his lap,
        unmoved by her despair,

        and he can't even bring himself
        to roll down the window.

        She looks at him desperately, pleading,
        and then runs into the woods where the assassins,

        in brown trench coats, hunt her down
        and shoot her several times.

                                        What the hell!

She collapses, finally, onto the snow-covered
ground, blood on her face. The film has that
particularly washed-out, bleak mood and look.
A flat '70's technicolor which perfectly fits
        (the scene of)
the Creve Coeur picnickers, the overcast sky,
the red and white checkered Imo's pizza boxes.
Seriously? no one brought anything

                       except Imo's and beer?
A cartoon, a wholesome picnic basket, a thought bubble.

The picknickers laugh at the Falls
and mock the dudes in their pickup trucks.
A group of walkers appear from nowhere.

Walking   —

>The power walker is winding down his exercise
>for the day:
>>*I think I'll go straight to the store*
>>>*and get some things for dinner—*
>>*what'll it be . . . Schnucks or Dierbergs?*

>>In Creve Coeur, Dierbergs is the rival
>supermarket to Schnucks. D-i-e-r-b-e-r-g-s.
>Both names are German but Dierbergs
>has a softer sound,

>and rolls of the tongue, unlike the harsh S-c-h-n-u-c-k-s.
>According to legend, Dierbergs was once a charming
>General Store, an early Creve Coeur grocery pioneer.

>In the '60s, every late-summer Dierbergs
>proudly stocked bright red plump tomatoes
>from local farmers, at a time when grocers were barely
>stocking *any* fresh produce, save a plastic-wrapped head

>of iceberg lettuce and a bin of some onions.
>Dierbergs has marked time
>by expanding a flagship location—
>the DVD kiosk, the bank, the florist,
>the pharmacy, the tobacconist,
>the café with cooking classes.

>>Don't get me wrong,
>Dierbergs is a popular chain of supermarkets now,
>but this one in Creve Coeur is the original

                                        since the 1850s,
         though you wouldn't know it by looking
         at the small shopping center attached: Verizon,
         Birkenstock & More, The Great Frame Up,
         Tuesday Morning, Clarkson Eyecare . . .

Much more than at Schnucks, the Dierbergs deli counter
is super popular and that's mostly because of Bob's
barbecue sauce! Customers talk about it a lot.
You can pick up your own bottle or get the actual bbq meats
in the hot deli section already basted
                                        in Bob's sauce:

a whole chicken, slabs of ribs,
                    pulled pork, pulled chicken, and salmon.

Down the block from Dierbergs
                                is Denny's restaurant.
They have large windows that look out onto
the parking lot,

                    not ordinarily offering much of a view:

a couple of bushes and a yucca plant
surrounded by rocks in a small, landscaped strip.
But around noon one steamy Thursday in July,

                            two MRI lab technicians
from Metro Imaging West County walked in

                                        for lunch
and were seated at the window table overlooking
the bushes.

Something caught their attention!

                                          Amid
the greenery, peeking out from beneath
the yucca plant was a human skull.
It wasn't the pearly color of an anatomy-
class specimen

                                    or haunted-house prop.
It was a shade of ocher, with bits of dirt
lodged between its teeth.
The face of the skull, jawbone askew,
was aimed directly at the window!
One of the women thought it must be a prank.

She called the manager over and pointed it out.
                                  The manager immediately

pulled down the blinds, and then called the Creve Coeur
police. Within the hour, crime-scene investigators
arrived, photos were taken, and the skull was sent
to the medical examiner's office. IT DON'T MATTER

WHERE YOU BURY ME, I'LL BE HOME FOR DINNER AND TV.

II.

Someone
       posted this corrective to the legendary Creve Coeur
namesake:

Actually, the lake was named Lac du Creve Coeur, or Lake of the Broken Heart, and was named by Pierre Laclède, who was among the Jean Pierre and Augustus Pierre Chouteau party, exploring the area and setting up trading treaties with the local Native Americans

*for the fur business in the newly founded village
of Saint Louis around 1760—*
              he gives no reason for the sorrowful name.

Someone else posts:

This gets fun for me since I am a direct descendent of these people and can go first-hand, so to speak. The Misura tribe [Missouria] camped on the upper picnic area off Marine Ave., and the story my grandmother Hazel told me was . . . in the 1700s, Pierre Laclède—who was basically the founder of St. Louis—and a Native American woman supposedly fell madly in love. The Chief refused to allow them to marry (this is a typical story told about many midwestern names, especially lakes) and the woman threw herself off the cliff and died.

           *Well, it DID NOT happen where the sign is . . .
           but north at the bluffs.*

           I have Madame Chouteau's Bible!

*It has notes in it about this event. So, the story goes . . .
apparently Laclède was so upset about her death
that he named the lake LAC DU CREVE COEUR.*
                              *I have seen many websites
that put the story down, and in most areas*
                              *it is just that,
a tall tale. But my family does have the letters and the Bible
to back up our story on this lake.*

      Up here.
           A cop points
              to a sign nailed
      to a tree: *here lies the city!*

           And here lie the future
children in it—even, or especially, the one who says
he has something bad in his head that won't come out.

Walking   —

                              instead
of driving—to the Creve Coeur AMC 12 for a Sunday
matinee is a treat. Once, in July, on a hot afternoon,
a guy sitting next to me in the theater stood up and recited
the Lord's Prayer! I thought he should be removed
from the theater. I started looking around for some help—
everyone just looked baffled or slightly nervous.
For sure, the awkward vibe

of sitting next to this preacher guy absolutely
influenced my experience. I kept imagining that he might
jump up again and evangelize something or, worse,
whisper something

              about his savior Jesus Christ into my ear,
or worse still, get crazy or violent.

                      The movie was *Quantum of Solace*
which was already stressful because of the nonstop action,

               so I didn't need this added element of suspense.
I was leaning away from his seat so hard that I left with
a neckache. When the movie was over and everyone
got up to leave, the worshipper stood up and just started
to file out

            like everybody else, like nothing had happened!

Take a deep breath. You only have one shot.
Make it count. I don't think the dead
care about vengeance .   .

    .   .   .   .

CREVE COEUR—A St. Louis-based developer has plans to buy portions of Bayer's (formerly Monsanto) Creve Coeur campus as the agribusiness giant moves to create a hybrid working environment. Pier Property Group is partnering with Edwardsville-based Fireside Financial on the deal to acquire the Bayer's offices in Creve Coeur. Pier Property Group declined to comment. Fireside Financial said the property will be redeveloped as a mixed-use project: "We're looking forward to bringing exciting new features to the Creve Coeur market." Bayer's sprawling campus long served as Monsanto's headquarters before Germany-based Bayer bought the company in 2018. "Like all companies, Bayer continually evaluates the facilities we utilize to ensure we're able to best meet the needs of our customers and employees. As working from home becomes more prevalent as a result of new technology and the pandemic, we envision a future that will require less physical office space than before," a spokesman said. Bayer's spokesperson went on to reiterate that the former Monsanto Headquarters should be treated like a landmark.

    Look, all these boxes of puzzles?

                              Why did dad frame *Barn Owls*,
or *Horses in the Meadow,* or *Bedtime Kisses?*—
which is a mama bear and her cub

kissing at sundown as they sit near a moonlit lake.
And *Land of Freedom* (dad, really?)
which features fierce looking bald eagles
soaring across a dramatic sky
and wispy American flag
       silhouettes blowing in the background?
I just like eagles, he shrugged. And three of those
                            Baby Tooth Survey cards!
Pinned on each card is a red and white button that reads:

I gave my tooth to science.

                        A cheerful cartoon of a boy
with a mop of hair and a gaping smile
proudly showing his missing front tooth.
Each card contains the child's biographical information,
township, and batch number.
The image of a tooth fairy, like Tinker Bell,
with a wand sprinkling fairy dust
over the futuristic image
of an atom.

          Later, when I told my older brother
about finding the Baby Tooth Survey cards

                            he recalled
all the details about the nuclear testing in the area
and how scientists learned that exposure
could be gauged by looking at children's baby teeth:

> *It has something to do with drinking milk*
> *and the radiation exposure in the cows!*
> *The alarming rate of radiation and childhood*
> *cancers worried mom and dad a lot.*
>
> *I voted Barry Commoner of the Citizens Party*
> *for President in 1980,* he told me, *because of*
> *his involvement in that Baby Tooth Survey.*

      I told him I found his hockey stick,
a cowboy outfit, and a science lab kit if he wanted any of them.

 An atomic tin lunchbox pail with a red swinging handle and graphics depicting astronauts in space wearing their suits and space helmets floating from their rocket ship while surrounded by stars, alien spaceships, and Planet Earth in the corner. In dark cobalt blue the phrase: *Lift-off*.

The preacher said: *Give up your money!*
In bad weather, the power walker retreats
to the Saint Louis Galleria for an indoor walk in the mall.
It's the best shopping mall near Creve Coeur and the wide
halls are known to be walker friendly.

      The power walker touches
his toes and manages an abbreviated version of his stretches.
At the atrium entrance, there's a preacher
going on about the sins of consumerism. *Amen!*

        Amen! Amen!

He preaches that we don't need to buy new things
but we need to give to others. *Amen!*

                    We need to give up the material
world and invest in the spiritual world.
Two security guards in ill-fitting company suits
hustle over to the preacher

whose sweet voice is projecting through the mall.
He says that the lessons of the Bible are the opposite

        of how we live our lives, that we bury
        our heads in the sands of fancy products,

                    we feel nothing for our fellow man!
We just buy things to make ourselves feel better.
Quickly, the security guards grab the preacher by his elbows.

He goes quietly. *That preacher is not totally incorrect.*
The walker reflects, as he settles into a reasonably brisk pace.
Look around! Also, the power walker is impressed
by the preacher's knowledge of economics:

according to the Federal Reserve, stated the preacher,
39 percent of Americans don't have the cash on hand
                    to cover a $400 emergency.
And more than half of American households
couldn't live without their income for just one month!
        The power walker considers his own
economic forecast and arrives

                    at a different conclusion:
too many of us prioritize the present over the future.

  The Delmar Divide refers to Delmar Boulevard as a dividing line running east-west across St. Louis City and County. In the early twentieth century, the St. Louis real estate industry employed a system of racial covenants and steering to drive the city's growing Black population to neighborhoods north of Delmar, while driving white families to the west.

Welcome to Creve Coeur!

In 1916, St. Louis became the first city in the nation to pass a racial segregation ordinance by voter referendum. It was nullified the following year thanks to the Supreme Court, but St. Louis realtors and developers simply reverted to the use of racial steering to enforce the Delmar Divide. In the 1930s, as part of FDR's New Deal, the federal government began to subsidize and incentivize home mortgages in an attempt to kickstart the economy. To guide the incentives, the federal government hired local squadrons of appraisers, brokers, realtors, and other real estate professionals to designate areas as "best," "still desirable," "definitely declining," or "hazardous." The areas deemed hazardous were overlaid or outlined in red, giving rise to the term "redlining."

After a satisfactory indoor workout,
the power walker winds down by window-shopping.
Around the holidays, the Words of Wisdom bookstore
is bursting with religious articles:
hand-crafted nativity crèches, Bible story
porcelain figurines, and colorful Christmas story books
with catchy titles like:

At Home With the Word!

In front of each top-selling religious book,
he notices framed author photos:
men with neatly styled gray hair,
nuns in their habits.

No similar calm next store
where the iLoveKickBoxing Gym pounds
energetic music from the entrance.
The preacher, somehow, has remained in the mall.
The power walker recognizes him, nods,

and the preacher approaches with a broad smile.
They look on together at the window display

of religious articles—the preacher points back
to the kiosk booths in the hallway wing:

> *Look at this one*
> *selling phone plans.*
>   *It's fascinating*
> *as real estate, right?*
>   *I gotta admit*
> *I'm somewhat interested.*
>   *My wife and I*
>
> *have been hatching*
>   *at least one*
> *entrepreneurial idea*
>   *of our own.*
> *She's been playing around*
>   *with making soap.*
> *It's a darn good product—*
>   *probably*

                                we could
market a whole line of handcrafted soaps—
just wondering what the rent is on one of these stalls . . .

                            I got laid off
but, I mean, why should I move from Creve Coeur?
I grew up here and my parents moved here from downtown
before that. A lot of family history here, but I just wish
the outlook was better for good paying jobs.
There's no money in preaching at the malls,
and I don't have the cash to start my own church
or anything like that—I don't need much, just the Lord
by my side, like I said, but you know how it is.
Anyway, on another note all together,

do you know anything about private banquet rooms?
My brother has been suggesting we do a big family
holiday party. Everyone is in town this year, and he mentioned
going to a restaurant. But here's my question: should we book
a banquet room or just get a large table at a restaurant?

I don't care for the attitude of a private room, but I suppose
that's what everyone prefers. Nobody is saying that,
but I have a sense that, at the end of the day,
we'll probably just go to Aunt Helen's,
as usual, because I come from a family of tightwads!

We know a lot of you have wondered about those booths you see in your shopping malls, but you don't know who to ask about renting one yourself. Well, in the commercial leasing industry, they're called Specialty Leasing units. Specialty Leasing in the retail space is the industry name for short-term retail space leasing in malls, shopping centers, and other retail centers.

RMUs (Retail Merchandising Units), retail carts, mall booth rentals, kiosk space, and pop-up shop leasing all fall under the Specialty Leasing category and are intended to add short-term retail space and more flexible leasing options for businesses as well as increase the variety of retail selections and spaces available to consumers within the mall space. Specialty leasing is a great option for smaller businesses looking to get off the ground with a more short-term, less expensive, and flexible option as well as for larger businesses looking to gain a more well-rounded exposure to shoppers throughout a mall.

Grow your brand and reach a larger consumer audience with help from our Specialty Leasing property management team. Showcasing your products in a pop-up shop can generate interest among shoppers who are already in the mood to buy. Whether you're a first-time retailer or an experienced merchandiser eager to showcase a seasonal assortment, our shared-space short-term Specialty Leasing opportunities are designed to fit your business needs.

Part with their money?

— the preacher goes on,
not my family! Do you think any one of them

will step up and offer to help me out? Not on your life!
But they'll buy over-priced Christmas gifts all day long!

                    In winter, the Creve Coeur Falls freezes
over with its thick slabs of white ice, like stalactites.
The whole scene is gray, as expected, nothing like
the marvelous blue and pink stage lighting projected
onto the stalactites and stalagmites of Meramac Caverns,
where an Ethel Merman recording of *God Bless America*
blares out from a loudspeaker on a continuous loop
at the conclusion of each cavern tour.

    The following Sunday, the walker is back
on the trail powering above the Creve Coeur Falls.

                    Just a little snow
is no obstacle . . . nothing beats the great outdoors.
He crushes a twig under the frost along the path.
What separates a twig from a monster?
Some kind of joke? The Falls is not amused, it mumbles:

I am not a man. I am a broken-hearted
infant or ancient rock formation.
I am not a riddle waiting for the future.
The Falls answers to all nomenclature:
Dripping Springs, the Creve Coeur Waterfall, The Bluffs.
Historically speaking, these are not the designations
that trouble the Falls. A small chip of limestone
                    drops into the basin below—
empty cans floating under the pedestrian stone bridge.
                                          Amen.

Amen! Amen! Let's consider that new vehicle.

*The Creve Coeur Weber Chevrolet
dealer always ranks the highest
on service. I originally made
phone contact with Ed Burns*

*advising him of my interest
in a vehicle which was noted
to be at their dealership.
Ed not only confirmed*

*the truck was there
but also gave me all the valuable
information right over the phone.
I went ahead and made the purchase*

*sight unseen.
Once I was able to arrive
at the dealership, Ed had
the vehicle already cleaned,*

*fueled, and ready to go.
He made sure the truck
was exactly what
I was wanting!*

*What happened next kind of amazed me. As I was working through
the financials, Ed called me over to demonstrate the basics
of the electronics inside of the truck and . . .*

when I turned around, the financing was done!

*The whole deal took less than twenty minutes
with no pressure to buy anything extra.
How many times does that happen. Like never!
We've all had that experience when we buy a car*

and then here comes the hard sell for the extras.
I had none of that. I would definitely 100 percent recommend
working with the Weber Chevrolet Dealership . . .

                                            Weber dealership replies:
Ryan, we can't thank you enough for your wonderful review,

and for your referrals and recommendation!
It was a pleasure to assist you!
Thanks for being a part of the Weber Family!

        Ryan was happy. It was true.
        Ryan had to shout out loud that he was happy—
        happy with the truck,

        happy with his lot in life.
        He wasn't worried that the earth
        would one day open up

        and swallow him whole.
        On the drive home, the blessed Lord
        came to Ryan and put His hand

        on Ryan's shoulder and said . . .
        Ryan, all of this is yours!
        It comes with the truck.

(Gesturing towards the Creve Coeur horizon)
Yes! the traffic on Olive is horrendous.

                        Yes! the air smells rancid.
Yes! the vista is flat and uninspiring.

>   *Yes! the Creve Coeur official flag of the red heart*
>   *with a white crack is unwelcoming, but still, Ryan,*
>   *it all belongs to you now!* Ryan holds the wheel tight
>   as his new truck is lifted right off I-270 headed north,
>   drifting toward the clouds, eyes wide with awe, floating
>   above the crack of the heart-shaped lake.
>   *It's so true,* he says to himself, now drifting beyond
>   the clouds, *the lake does look like a broken heart.*

In 1917, East St. Louis was the scene of considerable racial unrest and labor strife in heavy industry. Employers, seeking a source of inexpensive labor as well as potential strikebreakers, advertised in Southern newspapers, promising Black employment and high wages if they came to East St. Louis. Approximately 12,000 Blacks arrived seeking work. Although hundreds of them found employment, more did not and this swelled the ranks of the jobless. East St. Louis was not prepared to handle this sudden influx of people. Social services and housing were inadequate.

When a union-called strike at an aluminum plant was put down in April 1917, the union blamed the strike's failure on the Blacks. Antiblack remarks made at a union meeting during the following month triggered a riot on May 28, during which several Blacks were beaten.

>   The Creve Coeur Lake is an oxbow lake,
>   meaning it was caused by another body of water,
>   in this case by the Missouri River floods.
>   The meander of the river creates a U-shaped body.
>   An oxbow lake is a stillwater lake, meaning water
>   does not flow into or out of them. These lakes often
>   become swamps or bogs—they dry up because
>   their water evaporates.

Conditions remained unsettled and tense throughout June, and, on the evening of July 1, a group of armed whites in an automobile drove through a Black neighborhood shooting into homes. The following day, the rioters took to the streets. According to the official reports, nine whites and at least 39 blacks were killed, hundreds were wounded, and more than 300 houses and 44 railroad freight cars were destroyed. A

St. Louis Post-Dispatch Staff Reporter writes: "For over an hour last evening I saw the massacre of helpless Black people at Broadway and Fourth Street, in downtown East St. Louis. Saint Bartholomew's day did not outdo this massacre. Indescribable barbarity was born on this moment. White boys of thirteen, fourteen, and fifteen were in the forefront of every felonious butchery: girls and grown women, wielding bloody knives and clawing at the eyes of dying victims, sprang from the ranks of the mad thousands. Each man, woman, or child slain was frightfully abused, and not allowed to die after being fatally pierced. They were kicked and beaten with fists, feet, and clubs, hanged, and shot some more.

I saw one of these victims, covered with blood and half conscious, raise himself on his elbow, and look feebly about, when a young man, standing behind, lifted a flat stone and hurled it directly upon his neck. This young man was much better dressed than the others."

> *No one really knows about this . . .*
> *I know about it*
> *because my father, uncles, and aunts lived through it,*
> Dhati Kennedy says.

Some refer to the incident as the East St. Louis Race War. Kennedy's father Samuel, who was born in 1910, lived in East St. Louis when the conflict occurred. By the end of the three-day crisis, the death toll was much higher than what was initially reported—many estimate that between 100-200 Blacks were killed.

"We spent a lifetime as children hearing these stories. It was clear to me my father was suffering from some form of PTSD," Kennedy recalls. "He witnessed horrible things: people's houses being set ablaze, people being shot when they tried to flee, some trying to swim to the other side of the Mississippi while being shot at by white mobs with rifles, others being dragged out of street cars and beaten and hanged from street lamps." Many residents of East St. Louis used the Eades Bridge—the bridge that connects East St. Louis, Illinois to St. Louis, Missouri—to flee.

> *Thousands were streaming*
> *across that bridge when what they called* the race war
> *got into full swing,* Kennedy says. *When that happened,*
> *the police shut down the bridge, and no one could escape.*
> *Some, in desperation, tried to swim, and drowned.*

Uncle Eddie and some of the other young men were armed—
he had a squirrel rifle. They staked out in front of our home

and warded off the marauding white mob
as they came down our street. They had to take cover
because the white men were shooting at them, Kennedy says.
There was a standoff if you will, and I understand
from my uncle that it seemed to last for hours.
They witnessed the burning of homes and people . . .
By early Monday morning, the whole neighborhood was on fire.
Kennedy's family decided to run for the river.

According to my uncles, it took four hours to get across that river.
They fashioned a raft out of old doors and charred wood
to cross the Mississippi River and get to the St. Louis side.
My uncles said they had to stay on the Missouri side of the river,
and in the east the horizon was just glowing for weeks
from burning buildings. For days afterward, you could still
hear screams and gunshots, Kennedy says.

The Creve Coeur Park information plaque details
a geological story. Some moisture seeps in under
the plexiglass fogging up the Points of Interest text:
The bluffs you see overlooking the lake were carved out
by the Missouri River over the course of thousands and
thousands of years. But in the 1950s, the lake almost dried up.
Luckily, the Missouri River rose the next year
to avoid any greater
                              despair!

W.E.B. Du Bois: "St. Louis sprawls where mighty rivers meet—as broad as Philadelphia, but three stories high instead of two, with wider streets and dirtier atmosphere, over the dull-brown of wide, calm rivers. The city overflows into the valleys of Illinois and lies there, writhing under its grimy cloud. The other city is dusty and hot beyond all dream—a feverish Pittsburg in the Mississippi Valley—a great, ruthless, terrible thing! It is the sort that crushes man and invokes some living superman—a giant of things done, a clang of awful accomplishment.

Three men came wandering across this place. They were neither kings nor wise men, but they came with every significance—perhaps even greater—than that which the kings bore in the days of old. There was one who came from the North—brawny and riotous with energy, a man of concentrated power, who held all the thunderbolts of modern capital in his great fists and made flour and meat, iron and steel, cunning chemicals, wood, paint and paper, transforming to endless tools a disemboweled earth. He was one who saw nothing, knew nothing, sought nothing but the making and buying of that which sells; who out from the magic of his hand rolled over miles of iron road, ton upon ton of food and metal and wood, of coal and oil and lumber, until the thronging of knotted ways in East and real St. Louis was like the red, festering ganglia of some mighty heart.

Then from the East and called by the crash of thunderbolts and forked-flame came the Unwise Man—unwise by the theft of endless ages, but as human as anything God ever made. He was the slave for the miracle maker. It was he that the thunderbolts struck and electrified into gasping energy. The rasp of his hard breathing shook the midnights of all this endless valley and the pulse of his powerful arms set the great nation to trembling . . . "

III.

*Many a tear
has to fall,*

*but it's all
in the game . . .*

Creve Coeur
is blessed

with an abundance
of limestone

exposed
at the surface

and buried
in the subsurface.

The Falls can tell
you all about

limestone erosion.

Winter is already here; the sidewalks are covered in ice
and the opportunities for power walking are fewer.

The implicit documents
>> just as the explicit documented.
>>>> Remember
the man at the Schnucks
>> Service Counter—they wouldn't
>>>> even
sell him a money order and he was trying to pay for it
in cash!
>> Whatever new spaces open
>>>> don't stay open for long—

the luster
>> of a new shopping mall's
>>>> *Grand Opening*
dulls in a couple of weeks.

No problem. *Any workout is better than no workout at all—*
the power walker laces up.
>> He dresses in layers
>>>> and braces for a cold rain,
powering through
>> his subdivision, admiring
>>>> a split-level house he once
looked at, put in a bid for, but lost out.
I remember that house,

he comforts himself, *looking a bit better*
>> *than it does today—maybe*
>>>> *it's my memory,*
maybe the owners
>> *don't keep it up . . . seen better days.*
>>>> *Walking downhill*

is, counterintuitively, harder than
>> *walking uphill, but uphill has*
>>>> *a greater sense*
of accomplishment.

Today was a downward spiral
                        made up of fears and
                                  no sense, at all, of accomplishment—
this whole business of a new awakening is more
                                  like a business
of despair.

    For what, asks the Falls, *am I still standing here for?*
For whom? I want no part
       of your loathing, your secret cabals,
                                  a descent follows
endless and destructive.

Listen! —

       it's been raining
                     cats and dogs
       over here, our whole deal
       flooded over . . . gone!

       Everything is in clean-up mode
       this morning at Schnucks because
       during the flash flood,

       there was a main
       sewer pipe break
       along the creek behind the supermarket—
       wastewater poured, knee-high,

       into the Schnucks on Olive Blvd.

       Apparently, a temporary pipe installed
       two months prior was damaged by debris
       during the flash flooding.

An estimated 50,000 gallons
of wastewater overflowed into Schnucks.

                                                      Unleashed!

damaging mostly the fish, dairy, and frozen food
sections.

There were warning signs
all over Creve Coeur, advising
the public of the overflow.
A force main sewer is a pressurized sewer line
that uses pumps to transport wastewater.

Pumps and force mains are necessary when gravity alone
is not enough to move wastewater through flat areas
or over hills to a wastewater treatment plant.

   Much of Creve Coeur, including most of St. Louis County, is serviced by a separate sewer system with two sets of pipes: one for wastewater and one for stormwater. In the separate system, wastewater sewers are designed to carry wastewater from, for example, sinks, dishwashers, showers, and toilets. Stormwater should be absorbed back into the ground or carried to a nearby creek or stream.

                        In 1763, Pierre Laclède and Auguste Chouteau
found St. Louis to be an optimal location
for fur trading.

                   A century later, the Veiled Prophet
found downtown St. Louis to be the optimal location
for their July 4th debutante ball and accompanying parade,
in which a daughter of a local aristocrat rides in a float

alongside a mythical figure whose identity is obscured
by an elaborate veiled headdress—and for 150 years,
the public has been asking this question:
given the robes, masked identity, and the secret society
—isn't the Veiled Prophet really just a klansman?
In the annual parade, the first float carries
the representation of the King of the Jinns
and his attendants under umbrellas.
Second, The Fairy of Poetry and Romance
with two giraffe representations.
On the street are the torchbearers carrying lanterns.

        The Veiled Prophet is sometimes
referred to as The Grand Oracle and the identity
    of any given year's leader

has been kept a secret. However, a 2021 report
publicly disclosed

    many of the executive officers.
Among them are some of St. Louis' most powerful
businessmen and dynastic patricians including:
Desloge (lead mining), Kemper (banking), Busch
(beer dynasty), and Schnucks (grocery store magnate).
        A few blocks away, the Delmar Divide

—flowers, and everything else, uprooted.
A dirt field, candy wrappers, an empty six-pack
of Busch Light—the sound of refreshment!
The power walker looks up at the clear morning sky:
it's the quietest place on earth.

    Another whisper, is it a whisper?
is it anything at all?—goes unheard.
    The Falls is not disillusioned about its less than

grand appearance—nothing compares to Niagara Falls,
or Cumberland Falls, or the Great Paterson Falls.
And if they do listen

*in the bramble or on the bridge
or near the lake, what*, the Falls wonders, *is it that they hear?*
The limestone façade of the Falls is soft and easy to carve into.
Somebody + somebody = forever.
The lake represents a tragic symbol of a broken heart,
but transcripts are hardly symbols.

*The Hearings of the House Select Committee
That Investigated the East St. Louis
Race Riots of 1917:*

Mr. Rodenberg —
> *... and the highest number that they ever saw together
> in one mob was about 2,000, and that the actual work
> of destruction and murder was done by about 500?*

Ms. Queen —
> *Yes ... and everyone knows the threat is still all around
> the city and as soon as the soldiers are removed ...*

The Chairman —
> *Have you any idea who the leaders of the mob were?*

Ms. Queen
says she does know some but *the point about the matter is this,
that the larger number of those murdered were not men,
but women and children.*

Shortly after the massacre, investigative journalist, educator, and early civil rights activist Ida B. Wells-Barrett wrote a series of investigative reports for the *Chicago Defender*—comprised mostly of interviews with massacre victims and damning evidence of the roles of the police department and the National Guard. The series was later collected as a book: *The East Saint Louis Massacre: The Greatest Outrage of the Century*. In it, Wells-Barrett writes: "No one molested me in my walk from the station to the City Hall, although I did not see a single person of color until I reached the City Hall building.

   I accosted the lone individual in soldier's uniform at the depot, a mere boy with a gun, and asked him if the governor was in town. When he said no, he had gone to Washington the night before, I asked how the situation was and he said, 'bad.' I asked what was the trouble and he said, 'The [Blacks] won't let the whites alone. They killed seven yesterday and three already his morning.'"

     A St. Louis couple makes headline news
standing in the driveway of their palazzo-style mansion
pointing firearms at demonstrators who were marching
unarmed, peacefully, to the mayor's nearby home.

Their anger mounted. Their faces red.
He was wearing a mustard-stained polo shirt, holding
an AR-15 rifle and she in a striped blouse, hand on hip,
waving a pistol. They shouted: *get out!* and *private property!*
This is a gated community with opulent houses—
French, Tudor, and Italianate—built to impress during
the grand 1904 World's Fair, only a few blocks, today, from
some of the most neglected areas of downtown St. Louis,

a few blocks from the once
highly regarded Soldan High School
where my parents, at sixteen,
                      first met in the library.

And She   —

    *they smashed through the historic
        wrought iron gates of Portland Place, destroying them,
    rushed towards my home . . .*

The gate was damaged at some point but none of this was confirmed.
                                          Later, on
                                  the evening news
                                          they said
                                          they thought
                                                they
                                          would be

                                                        murdered.

Soldan now ranks 348 among the 358 high schools
                                  in all of Missouri!
Less than two miles away is the prestigious Clayton School District
ranking in the top one percent in nearly all categories—*nationally*.

                                  The Falls can chronicle
the decline. The descent hastens
the ascent

        and other empty places—laces
in eyelets, why it's sure
                you were going to be left alone.

Cold winter days, the quiet of the snow. The only sound around
is a woodpecker drilling out a hole.

Go home. Write. Compose.

Ha!

Does everyone say: *it is what it is*
or only in certain places?

Ha!

  —an insistent pecking in the hickory tree.

And She —

  We feared for our lives!

  On KMOV TV, they were described as local heroes
  and the story went viral. They dressed as celebrities
  and pretended to be Bonnie & Clyde for a week.
  The ascending local news cycle, the failing
  memory . . . is its own sadness. The Falls grumbles:
  all day and all night, I look out over this broken-
  hearted lake and no one can tell you what that means

  and no one can even try . . .

 The white St. Louis couple who attracted national attention for brandishing guns at protesters will be back in the spotlight next week as speakers at the Republican National Convention . . .

       Forget it! You don't need my
 outstretched arms to envelop you.

 Cloudy skies early, then off and on rain showers overnight. Low 47F. Winds light and variable. Tomorrow will continue to be overcast with light rain developing later in the day.

    Favorable policies . municipalities
    top-notch school districts . Clayton, Ladue
          outstanding lawns .

  Mark McCloskey announces candidacy for US Senate seat:

He   *God came knocking at my door last summer . . .*

She   *. . . disguised as an angry mob—it really woke him up.*

A few years earlier, I was visiting my parents
at the Brentmoor retirement community: a converted
'60s high-rise building, not very fancy like the Gatesworth
next door with its manicured ponds, fountains, and gazebos.
As the elevator doors open, each floor of the Brentmoor
is graced with a Hollywood poster of a movie star
so residents can more easily recognize their floor.
Theirs was the John Wayne floor,
which pleased my dad to no end.

                    Next door
to their apartment is the compactor room

with stacks of newspapers for recycling—
a caption read: *a mother drops rose petals
                    over bloodstains.*

August heat is just as miserable in downtown St. Louis
as it is in Creve Coeur. But, in fact, in terms of worst cities
for humidity, St. Louis doesn't even make the top ten.
It always does for violent crime.

It's not the heat, it's the humidity, St. Louisans like to joke.
Once I left a few vinyls in the back window
of my mom's Ford Maverick for three or four hours
and they melted, literally.

Groceries will spoil in the trunk or the backseat
after a few hours. The fastest foods to spoil? —
avocados, fish, raw meat, berries, mushrooms, carrots.
If you leave a dog in the car with the windows up,

someone will call the police in a heartbeat—and obviously
if a child is left alone in a car seat for even one minute . . .

So, yeah, my dad was in the Army Reserve. He went to Fort Collins for training, and he described how everyone slept in barracks somewhere but then would go to work in a downtown St. Louis office. His job was—this was the early '60s—transporting or managing a bunch of early IBM punch-card computers. But these Army Reserve guys never did any work, just goofed off. He was telling me that one of the baseball Cardinals—Tim Something, Tim McCarver—was there with him. But they never did any work. They always goofed off. So, anyway, my dad met Tim McCarver in the Army Reserve. McCarver, of course, was on some of those really great St. Louis Cardinals teams with Bob Gibson, Curt Flood, and Lou Brock. I think Lou Brock went on to have a car dealership in Creve Coeur. No, wait, that's Lou Fusz—the Lou Fusz dealership on Olive and Ballas. I have no idea what happened to Lou Brock. That's funny that I tried to give him a car dealership.

I don't know why, but when I think of St. Louis or Creve Coeur, I think of all the local foods that you can't get anywhere else. Like the St. Louis toasted ravioli. These toasted raviolis are ok—and thanks for bringing them—but they don't taste anything like the real St. Louis toasted ravioli. Every so often, you'll see a toasted ravioli somewhere else, but it's usually cheese-filled and baked, not fried. The St. Louis version is always fried, fried to order—they're fresh fried. And they have to come with the red sauce, the marinara sauce, though I don't think we grew up with that terminology—I think it was usually just tomato sauce. And in St Louis it's almost always the meat filled toasted ravioli—some combo of beef, veal, and pork. Nine times out of ten, the toasted ravioli on any menu is the meat version. Occasionally, there's a toasted cheese-filled version on the menu, but it's rare and probably considered fancy. It's very strange how toasted ravioli is only a St. Louis thing. It's not like there's an Indiana or Rhode Island version. It's only St. Louis. It's not like barbecue, as an example. There's Texas barbecue and, of course, Kansas City and St. Louis and they all have very distinctive recipes or styles, but toasted ravioli is just a St. Louis thing.

How does a food become so prevalent? I mean, of course there's an origin story. There's the story of the accident—someone put a ravioli in the fryer by accident. That seems believable. There's a place on The Hill that claims to be the originator.

You can get them there frozen now, so they're all over St. Louis. But there are multiple origin-story claims; whereas Provel cheese, as an invention, has a clear originator and I think it's trademarked. It's interesting that you can't trademark or safeguard a recipe but apparently with cheese . . . I mean no one else is allowed to manufacture Provel, even though Provel, technically speaking, isn't a real cheese—it's a processed dairy product.

The last time I was in Creve Coeur, my sister was reminding me of the library on Lindbergh across from the upscale Frontenac Plaza shopping mall. Terrible story— maybe I'll get to that later. But this library was like an afterschool home for me. My parents would just drop me off and I loved it as a kid. It was a lot of alone time, and I needed it. It was a different era. My parents would just drop me off there alone and come get me hours later. Growing up in Creve Coeur, for me, was so much about being alone. I would happily spend hours looking stuff up. They had a decent comic book section and I'd look up authors and illustrators and cross-reference them all day long. Also, they had a great music library and I checked out a lot of LPs. They must have had a fairly hip music librarian because they had a lot of off-beat records. And they were free—the first law of attraction! At that age I was picking out records based solely on the album covers.

It was my first introduction to visual art. I remember the three record covers that made the biggest mark on me. The first one was *Trout Mask Replic*a by Captain Beefheart. It had a photo of a guy with a fish for a face, wearing a tall hat. Inside was the band in a thousand psychedelic colors—it's a masterpiece of design and it's not one record but two, which was kind of wild at that age! The music was unlistenable which was an added attraction. The second album for me was *Remain in Light* by the Talking Heads because it had this great thermal imagery on the cover. And then, the third one was by Miles Davis, *Panagea*, which is a '70s era Miles live album, but it has an amazing cover by the Japanese graphic designer Teruhisa Tajima. So that library was such a remarkable place to discover that. But I had no supervision so I could just get what I wanted. My parents thought this was all good. Even though I didn't understand a lot of this music, in the conventional way of understanding, I had certain impressions, and this is in reflection. It's not something I thought about at the time, when I think about moments that mattered or things that struck deep.

Once when I was a very small kid, Sun Ra was coming to St. Louis, and they had a story on the local news. And I remember hearing about a jazz man from outer space. He was going be playing in St. Louis. This is the early eighties. And they showed footage of the orchestra all in their outfits and Sun Ra was playing the piano. And then he gets up and he sits on the piano. I remember the sitting on the piano thing so clearly because it was such an opposite image of anything I'd ever known.

Another clear memory is going with my mother to the St. Louis Art Museum. And it was just the two of us. I used to have a thing that I did as a kid a lot, which was to just disappear. Like, we'd go to a shopping mall and I'd go hide inside of a clothing rack. I had a tendency to walk away. Sometimes my mom, or whomever, would find me right away. Other times, it would take too long to find me; I'd be scared to death and I'd reappear frantically looking for my mom or sister.

So I did that at the museum—suddenly I found myself all alone in one of their galleries. I'd lost my mom and I was looking for her, but then I saw a bunch of people going into a room, so I followed this group. It was like an empty theater with a bunch of musical instruments and a show started. Four guys came out and they sat down at a table and they started playing cards. They played cards for a number of minutes, and then each guy would walk to his station and start playing an instrument. It turned out that it was the Art Ensemble of Chicago. Oh my God. And I was watching it, totally engrossed, and then I felt a hand on my shoulder. I turned around and it was my very irritated mother and a security guard. They had found me, but I wouldn't leave. My mom actually stayed and watched it with me, which was amazing. Doubly amazing because we weren't families who went to cultural events. We went to the Municipal Opera in the summer, the Muni as it's called, but we weren't like arts people.

My mother grew up in Central Illinois, which is about an hour and a half away from St. Louis. We would go there when I was a kid, my grandfather died when I was four, but he had a partner or I guess a girlfriend—his wife died before I was born—and she was like my grandma. We would go to his house which was near a new-ish, like '60s, highway that runs near the town. And then there was the original road into the town and a small main drag. Everything along the original road had been dying. Every time I went there, places had just disappeared, businesses were killed by the highway. And then in the '90s, a new Walmart went up and that killed the rest of the town. Everything went down. And then the Walmart went down.

During the pandemic, my dad and my daughter took a drive there just to show my daughter where her grandparents used to live and all that sort of stuff. We took the non-highway route, the old route. It was like muscle memory imagining all of these old businesses, I was like: Oh, coming up on the left is . . . and that used to be . . . etc. That's the way that memory gets triggered by sight or artifact or something where it can bring you back into the whole thing. But there was nothing. Everything was gone. It was truly like a ghost town. And not that it was thriving in the '90s, but it looked abandoned. Gone.

But my dad grew up in downtown St. Louis, near Soulard Market. He and his brother, Donny, who was stricken with polio at age six and was in a wheelchair. When he was a teen, I guess, his family moved somewhere around Clayton Road before settling in Creve Coeur. Our house was in that strip between McDonald's, Dierberg's, Monsanto, and Schnucks. Dierberg's is very memorable for me as a kid because that was where we shopped. I went to high school with a kid from the Schnucks family. A real schnook. And my father knew a Schnuck—there are multiple Schnucks all around West County. I think he knew some of the Schnucks from when he was a kid. Those kids probably own Schnucks now like their parents before them. If you're from St. Louis, you stay in St. Louis and you do what your dad did, or you leave. Those are basically the two options. It's like when my dad gives me random reports on people I don't care about . . . people he bumps into at Schnucks or somewhere, parents of my old classmates kind of thing, and he's like: do you remember Todd Holder? He's a lawyer in his father's firm. Now it's called Holder & Holder. I'm like, of course it is. It's always strange when my father does that because I didn't know many people in high school.

When I was a junior in high school, I was diagnosed with leukemia. So, I didn't really even go to senior year of high school. It was the last day of tests, finals, in my junior year, and that's the day that I was so sick that, uh, it's a long story. But I basically got diagnosed and, and then so intense, really intense. I was taken first to St. Jude's Hospital in Memphis. St. Jude, the saint of hopeless causes. My case was not a good case. I was 17 years old with something called Acute Lymphoblastic Leukemia, which is usually for little kids. These protocols for treatment, though, are very political. Long story short, they sent me back to St. Louis to that battery of hospitals on Kingshighway, in the Central West End, mostly connected to Washington University Medical. I think it was just called the Children's Hospital back then. I had to live there for a while and then, you know, moved back home and went back and forth a lot every day, all this craziness. I had a very extreme chemo. In fact, these protocols I'm talking about, it's like a multi-year study. And then they take that information, and they say, well, this worked and this could work better. And then they change the protocol and then they study it. So it's always sort of like a fine tuning of things. Different places had different things.

And so it turned out that what I had was best cured by a specific medical protocol that they had to get special approval from like the National Health Institute. Some crazy shit. I can't remember. I also was like dying while they're talking about it. So I lived at home the summer after eleventh grade, all through what would've been senior year. And then in that senior year, I applied to NYU to a special thing—because you're supposed to either go to cinema studies or film since they're not the same department—I got a special scholarship to go to a hybrid thing between the two of them. I wasn't supposed to leave home, but no one could stop me—I had to get out of there.

It wasn't only that I was going to go to New York, but I just wasn't going to stay in Creve Coeur and be the cancer kid in bed at home. There was no way. And, um, so I came here and then the first year that I lived in New York, I was going up to 32nd Street to the NYU hospital building. And on Tuesdays, I would have dialysis and since my veins had given out years earlier, they had to give me a port, which is a little plastic insert that goes straight in so that they can stick needles in there. So, I had this medical device in a backpack, and I'd travel back and forth to the dorm where I lived on University Place. I'd go in my room with this backpack that had a motor in it that was pumping in this Kool-Aid red chemo. It made me delusional. I started hearing words in the motor telling me things, or whatever . . . from this motor in the backpack. It also sounded like I was carrying a senior citizen on my back up a mountain and they were just panting in my ear the whole time. It was a weird year. I don't think about it much at all now, or describe it much, but that's the short version.

But getting back to the cultural stuff I grew up with in St. Louis, because that was really the railroad out, the ticket out of Creve Coeur for me—all the music and art that made the world seem larger than West County. Do you remember the freeform radio station KDHX? KDHX played some weird things, a lot of Zydeco and Cajun for instance. As a kid, there were a couple of shows I listened to religiously. One featured these St. Louis lugheads on Saturday nights from midnight to 3am. They would play local indie rock and just make dumb conversation and take calls. And so I listened to that from maybe seventh grade to twelfth grade, like every weekend and would call in and stuff like that. And they were also related to a St. Louis cable access show hosted by a guy named Pete Parisi. They would have on some low-level St. Louis celebrities and also just some oddball people that I loved, including my barber named Big Daddy.

Big Daddy was a wrestler in the St. Louis wrestling scene that happened at Kiel Auditorium—that beautiful art deco building that was for wrestling and hockey and even the St. Louis Hawks when St. Louis had a basketball team in the '60s. Of course they demolished this beautiful arena, like so many great buildings downtown. Anyway, Big Daddy really was a hairdresser slash wrestler. And Pete Parisi was the guy with a cable access show called *World Wide Magazine*. He had this rotating crew of unusual people and, like I said, these St. Louis sub-celebrities. It was a whole world. And then there was a guy on Sunday nights named Gabriel. Gabriel was an older African-American guy who came on the bus from Illinois every week to the studio to do an old R&B show, sort of like juke music, Ike Turner type, all played from 45s dubbed to cassettes that he had made at home.

I want to get back to more on Pete Parisi's show later, but I think this DJ Gabriel had some career influence on early Ike Turner when he was in St. Louis. And here he was in his twilight years, which actually went on for a long time, as a sort of bumbling old guy who often showed up late to his own show with stories about the bus, and he played honking R&B at ten o'clock on Sunday nights. It was amazing music and there weren't any other ways to access it in Creve Coeur, so I loved this and tuned in regularly.

And then the other show was a show hosted by a Black Muslim DJ who played a spiritual and free jazz show. And it was also on Sunday nights, I believe. I discovered this show in eighth grade and listened to it for years. It's still on the air today, and my childhood best friend, a white Jewish guy from Creve Coeur, is the host. But, you know, once you move away from St. Louis, it's more difficult to tune in to these shows.

Lately, I'm only going back once or twice a year. Once a year is great. Twice a year is pushing it. You know, it's like I have family I could see, but I don't know if it's sort of a coldness in me or that I don't understand what family is, but it's like I know I should visit, but it's hard to pretend that I'm close with these relatives. I understand the point—that way back I was related to you—but does that mean I have to make a trip to St. Louis and try to see everybody who I'm not close with? I don't know.

Most of my relatives stayed within a ten-mile radius of Creve Coeur, like Chesterfield or Maryland Heights. It all looks the same to me, but it's funny to hear my relatives talk about the distinctions between suburbs. But, to me, suburbs are sort of amorphous and the county lines seem totally arbitrary. Some have very strong identities, whether that be race, religion—around Creve Coeur it was mostly religion and class.

My sister and I were just talking about all of the shopping mall stores that don't exist anymore, like Hickory Farms—they used to give out German sausage samples around the holidays. And spreadable cheese. This was at the old Galleria before it was called the Galleria. Maybe it was the West County Mall? I'm not sure. But next door to Hickory Farms was B. Dalton bookstore. That was another place where my parents used to just drop me off and then come back an hour or so later and pick me up. I don't think I ever really bought anything there. I'd browse. It was like doing reference research—I'd look at a book and then see if they had another book that cross-referenced the first one. They always had someone cool-looking working at the Information Desk—probably some literary-looking guy who was a grad student at Wash U. This one guy—lanky, brown wavy hair, shoulder-length, parted on the side, John Lennon glasses, flower shirt, light brown corduroy jacket—I think that guy started to recognize me because he was always there and I was always asking him questions. I must have been around twelve or thirteen, but he always took me seriously and would escort me over to whatever I was looking for.

At the end of the wing, there was Dillard's department store, which, I guess, used to be Famous-Barr. And then around the corner, towards the parking lot entrance, was Camelot Music—where I used my Bar Mitzvah gift certificates to special order the CD *Early Works* by Steve Reich because I wanted to hear his tape collage piece "It's Gonna Rain." And then on the way out to the parking lot was The Magic Pan—their gimmick was crepes. There was like a crepe fad for a while there. And maybe a French onion soup fad, too. The Magic Pan was notorious for the best French onion soup all over town. St. Louisans loved that!—unaware that they were reaching back to their French fur trapper roots. I don't remember hardly any ethnic restaurants at all in West County. In general, there were very few people of color in Creve Coeur when I was growing up. As a family, we had almost zero contact with people who didn't look like us. And, in fact, that was also true of my friend's families in Creve Coeur.

Let's stop there, getting tired.

A.

P.S. I wouldn't feel right if I didn't get back to Pete Parisi and the *World Wide Magazine* public access cable show. I wanted to get back to Pete and *World Wide Magazine* because recently, in 2020, 36 boxes of master reels showed up on some guy's front porch—Jim something, I mean, not just any guy, Jim had been archiving Pete's entire series. Apparently, the boxes arrived all moldy and uncared for. They were delivered by Pete's girlfriend's daughters after Pete's girlfriend, Linda, died in 2010. There's a whole crazy story there about Pete's paranoia and whether or not Linda locked him in a room so he couldn't get his meds and died . . . crazy stuff that I won't get into now but, yeah, the *World Wide Magazine* was a hypnotic portal into late '80s St. Louis. Weird name too: it was neither worldwide nor a magazine—in fact, it was hyper local. It was, at times, like great outsider art and at other times it could be just dumb or offensive like the sensibility in the movie *Jackass*. Very similar. But for a teenager in the suburbs who liked weird shit, it was totally addictive.

World Wide Magazine went on for about fifteen years, and put out an episode every month or so. At first, Parisi hosted the show as the city's cab-driver tour guide. He made fun of St. Louis, but concerned himself with the regular people he drove around. Soon, the show downplayed the cab element and took on the format of picaresque interviews with some horsing-around comedy skits. Usually, Pete took us late-night tube viewers through downtown St. Louis—already in a steep, long-term economic decline. It was a universe where the center of the earth lay between Grand and Gravois and was hosted by an ensemble cast of St. Louis characters ranging from locals on the street to St. Louis sub-celebs. I remember the first episode of *World Wide Magazine*—not even sure it was yet called that—an hour-long program recorded in 1985 called "Every Day I Use Up a Year's Worth of Luck." After a hand-drawn title screen, the first piece of footage reveals three pink Oscar Mayer hot dogs circling around in a toilet bowl. "Next time I eat hot dogs, I guess I'll have to eat them a little bit slower," Pete sighs. And then it cut to Pete eating one of the wieners and saying something like: "Eh, they were better last night." Thus, the chaotic, homegrown, offensive genius of *World Wide Magazine* was born.

A.

Dear R.:

I've been looking this over and everything sounds about right to me, except I do feel that our conversation about St. Louis cuisine got short-changed. As such, I thought to correct that. I think you know what I'm talking about . . . I'm talking about the St. Paul sandwich! It's basically a fried fish sandwich that you get on sliced white bread with tons of mayonnaise. Strangely, it's a Chinese restaurant thing. My mother used to take us to a spot in Rock Hill which is on Manchester near McKnight. She got the St. Paul sandwich there and just adored it. She insisted it was the best. And she also got it in another place over by the airport—I don't know why we would go that far for a sandwich but looking back it's admirable that she felt that passionate about her St. Paul sandwich.

A.

And just one last thing, since you ask . . . yes, you can share all of this. There's nothing here that I feel like I need to edit. I'm not sure how many people will actually want to read about weird public access cable shows and toasted raviolis, but please do.

Afterword

by Joe Milutis

: a local pride; spring, summer, fall and the sea; a confession; a basket; a column; a reply to Greek and Latin with the bare hands; a gathering up; a celebration; in distinctive terms; by multiplication a reduction to one; daring; a fall; the clouds resolved into a sandy sluice; an enforced pause; hard put to it; an identification and a plan for action to supplant a plan for action; a taking up of slack; a dispersal and a metamorphosis.

"a gathering up . . . a dispersal"

In February of 1916, in the Grand Ballroom of the Plaza Hotel in New York City, the European Art collection of silk mill magnate Catholina Lambert was put up for auction by order of the Paterson Safe Deposit and Trust Company. Lambert, who rose in prominence from a poor English immigrant to become the owner of one of the country's largest private art collections, was forced to sell off these assets as a direct result of the Paterson mill strikes. The collection would be "dispersed"—a favorite word and key concept of William Carlos Williams, who, during his formative years, would have been able to visit the collection on Saturday afternoons—but not before Catholina Lambert, so the legend goes, buried a few choice pieces from his collection in the hills of Garret Mountain.

"a gathering up . . . a dispersal"

The two motions of William Carlos Williams's *Paterson*, are, like breathing in and breathing out, the *gathering* of what has previously been dispersed and the *dispersal* of what has previously been gathered, a dynamic, an AMERICAN THEME even, that came to impact the very composition of his work, endlessly organized in bits in various envelopes, never hitting upon its ideal form until death overtook both the man and the poem. Like the catalogue for the 1916 auction of Lambert's castle gallery, which one can now find online (with quaint selling prices penciled in the margins), every textual "thing" that Williams collects contains an infinite regress of other text-things, subject to their own accretion and weathering. Between Italy and geology—a world of art. A snapshot is captured of this totality, a plenum of trajectories intersects with the optics of the author in the gravity of place. But the all of the Falls of Paterson is ultimately unspeakable.

"a gathering up . . . a dispersal"

I meet Rob Fitterman at Veselka in the East Village to discuss his interpretation/rewrite/translation/echo of Williams's *Paterson* as relocated to his own hometown Creve Coeur, Missouri. For if *Paterson* is the poem of "no ideas but in things," what happens when the poem itself becomes a "thing," subject to various transits and embargoes, repros and other poems. For Fitterman, Paterson's silk factories become the Pruitt-Igoe projects and Monsanto World Headquarters; power-walking and Schnucks Rewards Cards now "animate a thousand automatons." We are sitting in a Ukrainian restaurant that has resisted the fate of many businesses around us that have submitted to rapid change and gentrification—even more dramatic than is usual for New York City, given the toll of the pandemic—although we are not, for all that, outside history: there is a new mural on the wall by Arnie Charnick, a modernist and semi-surreal shattering of rubble and fire out of which a fist emerges, gripping the Ukrainian flag.

"a gathering up . . . a dispersal"

The definitive textual version of Williams's *Paterson* is the volume introduced and edited, with copious notes, by Christopher MacGowan. Fitterman suggests that I play the role of MacGowan in his rewrite, by introducing and framing the various triangulations between *Creve Coeur*, *Paterson*, and the impossible object of the modern epic. I'm glad I'm not playing Marcia Nardi, the failed poet whose letters Williams included in his poem, even though I knew each email I sent Rob during COVID, as we were discussing his evolving alter-epic, could have found its way into the poem with me as aggravated interlocutor, animated by middle-aged gossip and complaint. Instead—MacGowan, the authoritative gatherer of the entropic text, who in his Appendix B explains his task as editor: Williams's impatience with proofreading after the first limited editions, and later his declining health, prevented him from striking a version that was fully finalized and approved by the author himself.

Appendix B of MacGowan ends with the following hieroglyph, a bulwark against erosion, an incantation warding off misreading, a prayer to the patron saint of lost pauses.

Because of the irregular stanza form that is a central characteristic of Williams' poetics in *Paterson* it can be difficult to tell whether the end of a page marks the close of a stanza. In this edition the following pages end with a space:

3	10	11	13	18	19	20	21	23	25	26	27
29	30	31	33	36	37	43	44	45	46	47	50
51	52	54	55	56	57	60	62	63	64	65	67
68	70	71	72	77	78	79	80	81	82	83	86
95	96	99	100	101	103	104	106	109	110	113	115
116	117	120	121	122	123	125	129	131	133	136	140
141	142	149	150	151	153	154	155	156	158	159	160
161	162	165	166	167	168	170	174	175	176	178	179
181	184	190	191	192	195	198	199	201	207	218	228
230	234	235									

"a gathering up ... a dispersal"

We all have our various Patersons, localities where once we gathered, and from which we now have dispersed. Thus, we can hone in on the incisive materialities of Williams's *Paterson* as our own condition's ideal model, which to be seen rightly must be seen with exactitude. Or, in the spirit of conceptual writing, we should regard it as an invitation to do the same, to copy Williams's gesture, to find the uranium in every city, its dissonant valence in the pitchblende of the real. Fellow Patersonian Robert Smithson said that if every city was a copy of the Eternal City—Rome—there was something new, special, and entropic about Paterson. While the typical American city hearkens back to the Roman model—we can see this in the classical banks and courthouses that dot the eastern seaboard and provide some semblance of guarantee against the failure of the future by way of a kitschy aesthetic pact with the past—the "new" Eternal City instead pointed to the future ... but one that would never be, a ruin of that future, a "ruin-in-reverse." So that, from the ruin of Williams's *Paterson*, Fitterman's *Creve Coeur* emerges, destined, fatal, part of the epic of Paterson's never-arriving, ever-repeating, final form. Each version creates its own mix of frontier oddities clashing with contemporary aperçus, insights that can never overcome their dispersals. "A reply to Greek and Latin with bare hands."

OR: "power [walking] onto the sidewalk at Schnucks, onward past McDonald's and into a future."

"a gathering up ... a dispersal"

The goal of early twenty-first century conceptual writing was a performative exactitude, never touching the (textual) real while doggedly tracing it, in order to highlight the entropic force latent in every copy. Vocal proponents of conceptual writing distanced themselves from remix, collage, and translation, opting for the cool, uncreative reinstantiation of a changing same. After twenty or so years, we are witnessing a loosening, a Gothicizing, a dispersal of these earlier ideals. Fitterman's *Creve Coeur* follows the shape of books I and II of Williams's *Paterson*, but expends new material across it, both personal (gasp!) and political, like a jazz riff on the chords of a fake book, the splatter of a Pollock, or perhaps something more bathetic and postmodern. "Squeezed out, with design" . . . but framed at Michaels.

"a gathering up . . . a dispersal"

Of course, although Williams directly copied texts from historical societies, personal letters, old newspapers, they are marked by his tinkering. As well, these small-type passages are framed by Williams's own ejaculations and interjections. "You just can't make this stuff up," he seems to say. And, "This stuff is part of our makeup." This innovation comprises the greatest debt that conceptualism and documentary poetics owes to him, and which Fitterman continues in the age of Yelp reviews and YouTube comments. *"There are giant bugs FLYING AT MY FACE!"*

"a gathering up . . . a dispersal"

There still remains in Fitterman the shadow of bedrock, the unchanging layers of the past, whether atrocity or geology that can't be wished away by poetry. This feature is emblematized in the original *Paterson* by Williams's proto-conceptual sampling of the Artesian well at the Passaic Rolling Mill, a passage where Williams simply lists geological strata with their corresponding depths, foregoing any commentary or poetizing. Yet, Fitterman does not preserve a similar attitude towards the modernist "hardness" of things in the world, traced by an equally thingly poetics. Instead of the cosmology of the Falls, a self-checkout line. Instead of old man Paterson, a father kvetching about discounts. Here, the world is not made of things and things alone, but is parsed by labor and capital: the reality of things is not locked in the mind "past all remonstrance" but is instead a surface fashioned by "employment."

It is the mall and not the Falls that is the psychic center of the city.

"a gathering up . . . a dispersal"

At one point in the text, Fitterman highlights the Baby Tooth Survey, a collection, a gathering up of children's teeth done in St. Louis in the late '50s and early '60s as a means of monitoring the effects of nuclear radiation testing. It's one of those stories that first circulates as family legend, dispersing as hearsay, only much later found to be fact. What were once vague, possibly fanciful, and thus largely forgotten stories now have an odd solidity and provability online. However, not everything, even now, makes its way to the Internet. The proof is in the provolone, but Provel mystery cheese and St. Louis toasted ravioli retain their inscrutability and proper strangeness. The Baby Tooth Survey, like accounts of Williams's "triadic line" are surprisingly still sketchy when searched. So we continue to prove our belonging—our provolonging—through the oral traditions of the local, by upholding these ephemeral facts, whether banal or implausible: that Dierbergs had farmers' tomatoes long before fresh produce was an easily accessible thing, but also "No one really knows about this . . . He witnessed horrible things: people's houses being set ablaze, people being shot when they tried to flee, some trying to swim to the other side of the Mississippi while being shot at by white mobs with rifles." In the case of St. Louis' history of redlining and race riots, stories are circulated, though barely, despite being edited out of official historical accounts.

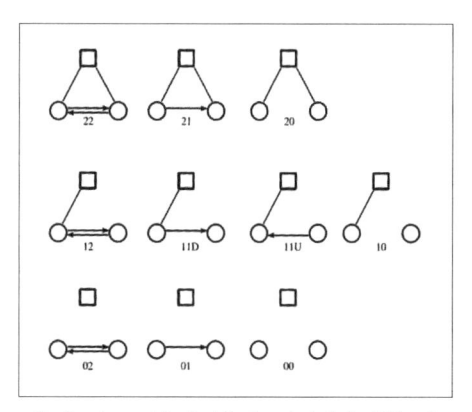

Top Google search for "look for the nul triadic line Williams"

"a gathering up . . . a dispersal"

I start writing this afterword while unexpectedly confined to my own hometown after an accident in Istanbul. With the combined help of and improvised rescue by a Princeton professor, a Syrian refugee, a Russian importer, and various family members, I was suddenly transported, gathered up from the chock-a-block of an ancient city on the Bosphorus to a hospital in the Lehigh Valley, a new modern complex located in a wide-open non-space that had once been farmland, situated at the nexus of highways outside the major urban centers so that even the nurses are hard-pressed to agree what city we are in.

Williams, of course, was the doctor-poet, his attentions shifting between the mending and the birthing of patients to his own impatient poems. One wonders whether it is a sign of his great patience or impatience when, in *Paterson*, he admits to peeling the label from a mayonnaise jar instead of attending to the torment of mothers in the waiting room. A doctor of the old school, however, he did show his impatience for the kind of modern corporate hospital where I now find myself. They are hospitals "with wings," a dubious metaphysical attribution in a place "where nothing / will grow." But here where I have been swiftly and inexplicably winged, instead of cinders and green bottle glass, there's a sunflower field and conference barn . . . supposedly. The former is past bloom, while the latter seems to have undergone some entrenched battles with zoning authorities, so, though its sign remains, it might not exist. It feels good to be suddenly in this corporatized ambiance seemingly without chaos and from my wheelchair, I keep prattling about how they have the best weather in the world here.

Fitterman's work has a dual-edged stance towards progress, in a way that I don't think the intentional flatness of his earlier poem "Directory" can merely be chalked up to anti-consumerism or anti-corporatism. *That preacher is not totally incorrect.* And yet, there is something to Creve Coeur that admits to a joy and even wonder, or at least the historical unavoidability of living within the corporatized spaces of suburban sprawl, despite the banality or even horror that subtends them. Fitterman power walks us through the Butterfly House and the carousel of Faust Park. Are they merely creepy tourist traps with a history that may be linked to

Goldman-Sachs, part of the Faustian bargain we make with the corporate for our creature comforts, or are they places where "wonder takes flight"?

Grasshopper statue in Chapultepec Park, Mexico City, mentioned in *Paterson Book II*, and monarch statue outside Sophia M. Sachs Butterfly House in Chesterfield, Missouri

Perhaps this is just what is meant by the sublime, akin to the homely wonders and uncanny surprises of what used to be called K-Mart fiction, which—we must give the devil his due—originated in the marvelous Zen-Yankee particularism of John Updike's own local musings.

"a gathering up . . . a dispersal"

Creve Coeur asks the question *Is memory always thanatoptic?* If the literature of memory gives off a rosy glow, death is always the firewood. It is a gathering up of dispersals. But how can one write of memory in spaces specifically constructed to inspire forgetfulness? The seemingly deathless and ahistorical promises of the mall, the corporate park, the megachurch, the medical campus, the non-site, the ruin-in-reverse, are now paradoxically sources of nostalgia. We see both the sources and sills of their disappointments, which were perhaps once ours but those past desires have now become strange. We no longer really want these things, or maybe we never did, because we know the cost, the cost. Long after their initial seductions have faded, we become aware of their implicit violence, but must live in the ruined infrastructure constructed for them out of the tyranny of small decisions. The failed trajectory of desire through its architectonic instantiations inspires Fitterman's power walk, which, as a bulwark against aging, seems in itself to be dated like aerobics VHS tapes. *Paterson*, but in the modality of vaporwave.

"a gathering up . . . a dispersal"

We'll get back to Fitterman's version of Paterson eventually, although since this type of work invites our own memories of gatherings and dispersals, a detour. And, in fact, the only thing I can remember about the pre-history of this general area around the new medical center is that it used to be the semi-rural and semi-forgotten backroads detour connecting downtown Bethlehem and west Easton, which was effectively the main road, before the highways were built. My grandfather would call the route "his BAILIWICKS," emphasizing the exotic word with a mixture of sarcasm and erudition that he lavished on $50 words.

He probably got the word from his favorite novel, James Fenimore Cooper's *The Last of the Mohicans*, which, now that I look it up (I haven't read it) might describe the tension-filled summer of 1757 in which Teedyuskung attempted to argue back stolen Lenape land in the courts of Easton, and the son of Chief Moses Tatamy was shot by a white teenager because he looked suspicious.

"a gathering up . . . a dispersal"

I eventually return to where this pointedly amnesiac, seemingly negentropic medical center does not hold sway, to the dense palimpsest of city where Teedyuskung made his claims, and which enjoyed extralegal status during Prohibition, so that its last boom was probably in the 1920s as a drinking town. You could get a bus here after the fights at Madison Square Garden in New York City to go drinking, either in the luxury hotel on the top of Weygadt Mountain, or for those of lesser means, various bootlegging operations, like in the basement of my Sicilian great-grandfather's grocery store. Here's where Pfizer, before it specialized in erection drugs and other pharmaceuticals, manufactured the color "rust." You would pass the reddened sheds and Quonset huts of Pfizer like a Martian terrain on the way to high school, while the particles of their pigment factory belched out over Route 22, across Cemetery Curve and into the cemetery itself, where the stately graves of old Easton are still stained by the Pfizer patina. There was an Italian ghetto right behind the factory where the housewives had to resign themselves to the fact that laundry whites placed on the clothesline would quickly become blood-colored by the pigment. They would also have to resign themselves to consequent cancers.

"a gathering up . . . a dispersal"

> What is the story, the myth again, the namesake?
> Tell it, please. Can it be told with pictures?
> Through The State Historical Society of Missouri?
>
> Their archives? County libraries? court documents?
> Can the story be told through transcripts,
> revised transcripts, revised interpretations?
>
> "Something else, something else the same."

When I am finally able to get back on my feet, their "limping iambics," I visit the Marx Room of the Easton Public Library. The name of this local history room is apt because here is the *materialization* of local history in what Williams called (at the beginning of Book III) the "cool of books." Williams alternately compares the books of the library to the "shelving green" of the locust tree and the acquisitive fortune of the art collector Samuel Putnam Avery. *Despite the library, how much information still goes missing*, both Fitterman and Williams seem to ask, or *what exactly IS the information that should be salvaged from the ruins of memory*? Books are as a wind "or ghost of a wind" through the leaves of the locust—and the *locus*. In the glassed-in corner of the Marx Room, I have gathered at my desk Indian treaties and 1950s infrastructure plans, Pennsylvania Dutch linguistics and Northampton County toponyms.

But there is one fact of history to which my attention is continually drawn, even though it has been almost invisible to me for half a century, yea, even though I had passed it, waited for rides by it, maybe even caressed its surface when, in the afterschool hours, I found myself in the library's lobby. It's a marble statue in a classical style of a boy with wild hair, ruff collar, in a kind of mini-skirt emblazoned with heraldry. His legs seem as if sprouted from winklepickers which open at the top, petal-like, against a background of acanthus. He's carrying (and one can barely read the inscription) a book of poetry. His eyes are rolling, almost petulantly.

It turns out this is a statue that Williams also would have encountered frequently in his youth, and it represents everything about art that he grew to hate.

"a gathering up . . . a dispersal"

There is no wall text for the statue, but I do an online search using some of the few barely legible inscriptions on the statue itself, then there it is. In the aforementioned *Catalogue of the valuable paintings and sculptures by the old and modern masters forming the famous Catholina Lambert collection removed from Belle Vista Castle, Paterson, New Jersey*, we find entry 383—*The Youthful Tasso*, by Lelio Torelli (Italian: Contemporary) sold for $250 to William Seaman, agent. What an itinerary, from Italy to Paterson, finally winding up by the umbrella rack at the Easton Public Library!

Here, done up in youthful finery, is the tortured author of the epic poem *Gerusalemme Liberata*. I am stunned by this discovery, but in the ensuing days gradually sickened by the realization that here was a poet, famous at eight years old, who spent his life in poverty, exile, and madness, who endured the meddling of jealous pedants and courtiers, only to die before receiving the recognition he deserved: being crowned the "king of poets" by the Pope on Capitoline Hill. Could this be the worst statue in the world? Pointedly European—baronial even—its gaudy sentimentality barely touches the reality of the life of the poet. Ultimately insulting to him. Tasso clearly comes off as a brat. Perhaps the intention was to glorify lost innocence, which may have appealed to Lambert, who lost all but three of his eight children to diseases now rendered obsolete by modern antibiotics. But it is the "modern," then, which should be taken up and glorified, we can now say with hindsight. One can imagine Williams looking upon this image in its weird hallway annex of the Lambert Castle gallery. In the only extant photograph, Tasso is poised among steel buttresses in what looks like a futuristic train station. I think Williams would have been more compelled by this almost science-fictional architecture, its international élan, than he was by the ruffled statue of a poet-clown.

"a gathering up . . . a dispersal"

When Williams, in Book V of *Paterson*, celebrates

> A WORLD OF ART
> THAT THROUGH THE YEARS HAS
>
> *SURVIVED!*

he is not talking about this type of stony artifact, but rather the ephemeral, implausible, and unprofitable antics of Dada and Surrealism.

"a gathering up . . . a dispersal"

I feel like I've made a great discovery, but the Marx Room librarian has gotten there first, just barely. She looked into the history of this strangely anonymous statue a year before, and she's gone further and has found that it is not actually a rendering of the epic poet Torquato Tasso, as the catalogue of the Lambert Castle collection shows, but of a minor character from a forgotten historical novel concerning a page boy's forbidden love for a Medici noblewoman. This new information leaves me strangely cold. She shows me an Italian *catalogue raisonné* of its sculptor, and it seems that up until very recently, those charged with the sculptor's legacy had no idea where the statue had got to, even though they still retained its black and white photo. The young sculptor sold it in 1878 while he was still in art school so that he could finance a trip to France (a journey that Williams would later pointedly eschew, although fashionable for artists of his generation, opting instead for Rutherford, NJ). It was lost sight of for over a hundred years, while I and others saw it quite regularly in the Easton Public Library lobby, by the umbrella rack.

Here's where we return at last to Fitterman and the world of conceptual art, and the ways in which *Paterson* has become *Creve Coeur*, its ruin-in-reverse or virtual continuance. It became clear to me that the silk baron, in a fit of creative arrogance, could have renamed the statue himself, and that renaming was the most resonant and interesting thing about the art. By this appropriation, we can imagine Williams was unconsciously or consciously affected in his youth, spurred to action and art by the inappropriate memorialization of a failed epic poet to eventually write his paean to the questionable status of memorialization itself, what Nancy Barry called "the fading beautiful thing of *Paterson*" and Williams "that God damned and I mean God damned poem *Paterson*." Eventually Fitterman would write his recoded and broken-hearted *Creve Coeur*, and eventually I would posit some words as well. *Event*ually, for art is nothing if not event, or evanescence, and if an epic of evanescence must paradoxically be done, must eventually be finished (even if the story can never quite be told), it is in order to leave things undone so that we can continue in these fundamental movements, this adventure of gathering up and then, with a sad joy, dispersing.

Acknowledgments

I have many people to thank for this book. I leaned heavily on my friends and fellow poets who read or listened to versions of the book along the way. I'm enormously grateful for their support. A big thanks to the following: Roberto Balò, Anselm Berrigan, Marie Buck, Lonely Christopher, Kevin Davies, Tim Davis, Mónica de la Torre, Al Filreis, Coco Fitterman, Lawrence Giffin, Alan Gilbert, Aurelia Guo, Josef Kaplan, Matt Longabucco, Holly Melgard, Rodrigo Rey Rosa, Kim Rosenfield, Noha Sadeq, Lisa Sanditz, Rodrigo Toscano, Aaron Winslow, and Joey Yearous-Algozin.

    I had the good fortune of having two close readers who, over the course of five years, read several drafts of this manuscript and shared crucially helpful notes: Joe Milutis, whose detailed comments and scholarship of *Paterson* were vital to me, and Steve Zultanski, whose encouragement went far and whose insights are now intertwined with my own. Thank you both.

    Generous excerpts from *Creve Coeur* were published in *Brooklyn Rail* and *Air/Light*—I am grateful to those editors and publishers.

    Special thanks to historian Walter Johnson for his revealing history of St. Louis, *The Broken Heart of America,* and to Christopher MacGowan for his revised edition of William Carlos Williams's *Paterson* (New Directions, 1992). *Creve Coeur* closely follows the stanzaic form of this edition. Thanks, also, to Phia Holland for her expert copy editing and Serena Solin for proofreading.

    I am indebted to my fellow denizens of Creve Coeur, Andrew Lampert and Henry Goldkamp, whose "letters" appear in this book anonymously.

    And, finally, thanks to Matvei Yankelevich for his meticulous editing, continued support of my work, and his tireless commitment to contemporary poetry.

ROBERT FITTERMAN's fifteen books of poetry include *Rob's Word Shop* (Ugly Duckling Presse), *No Wait, Yep. Definitely Still Hate Myself* (UDP), *This Window Makes Me Feel* (UDP), *Rob the Plagiarist* (Roof Books), *Holocaust Museum* (Counterpath), and the four-volume, serial work, *Metropolis*. His poetry is often composed of found texts that emphasize the personal relationship to social themes with broad critiques of cultural institutions and constructs such as chat rooms, consumer reviews, shopping malls, and museums. He is the founding member of the artists-poets collective Collective Task. He lives in New York City and teaches writing at New York University.

JOE MILUTIS is a writer and artist who teaches for the MFA in Creative Writing and Poetics at the University of Washington-Bothell. He has attached himself to poems such as *Paterson* and *Creve Coeur* in acts of extreme reading and experimental translation. He is the author of books, parabooks, expanded essays, and media-literary hybrid works, which can be found at www.joemilutis.com.

Creve Coeur
Copyright © Robert Fitterman, 2024
Afterword copyright © Joe Milutis, 2024

ISBN 978-1-959708-08-7
LCCN: 2024937408

First Edition, 2024 — 1200 copies

Winter Editions, Brooklyn, New York
wintereditions.net

Cover image: Donald Owen Colley, *Creve Coeur Falls in Winter*, 2024. Woodcut, 11¾″ x 11″, printed by ProppJonesStudio. Used by permission of the artist.

we is supported by subscribers and individual donors, and extends special thanks to recent Supporting Subscribers: Anonymous, Anonymous (in memory of the Beaubiens), Yevgeniy Fiks, and Elizabeth T. Gray, Jr. The author wishes to acknowledge New York University's support of this publication.

we books are typeset in Heldane, a renaissance-inspired serif designed by Kris Sowersby for Klim Type Foundry, and Zirkon, a contemporary gothic designed by Tobias Rechsteiner for Grilli Type. The layout and covers are done by the editor following a series design by Andrew Bourne. This book was printed and bound in Lithuania by BALTO print.

Winter Editions

Emily Simon, IN MANY WAYS

Garth Graeper, THE SKY BROKE MORE

Robert Desnos, NIGHT OF LOVELESS NIGHTS, tr. Lewis Warsh

Richard Hell, WHAT JUST HAPPENED

Marina Tëmkina & Michel Gérard, BOYS FIGHT
[co-published with Alder & Frankia]

Claire DeVoogd, VIA

Monica McClure, THE GONE THING

Ahmad Almallah, BORDER WISDOM

Hélio Oiticica, SECRET POETICS, tr. Rebecca Kosick
[co-published with Soberscove Press]

Heimrad Bäcker, DOCUMENTARY POETRY, tr. Patrick Greaney

Robert Fitterman, CREVE COEUR

Karla Kelsey, TRANSCENDENTAL FACTORY: FOR MINA LOY

Alan Gilbert, THE EVERYDAY LIFE OF DESIGN

Betsy Fagin, FIRES SEEN FROM SPACE

POSTCARDS FROM THE SIEGE, ed. Polina Barskova
[co-published with Blavatnik Archive]